JN328660

Product and Process
in the L1 and L2 Writing of Japanese Students of English

About the Author

Keiko Hirose is a professor in the Faculty of Foreign Studies at Aichi Prefectural University, where she teaches various undergraduate English courses as well as applied linguistics and TEFL to both undergraduate and graduate students. Her research interests include teaching L2 writing, comparing L1 and L2 writing processes, and contrastive rhetoric.

Product and Process in the L1 and L2 Writing of Japanese Students of English

Keiko Hirose

KEISUISHA

Copyright © 2005 Keiko Hirose
First printed in February 2005
Published by Keisuisha Co., Ltd.
1-4 Komachi, Naka-ku, Hiroshima 730-0041
JAPAN
ISBN 4-87440-862-1 C3082

Acknowledgments

I thank all those who contributed to the completion of the present volume. First of all, I would like to thank all the participants in the study for their invaluable cooperation. Mariko Murai, Toshihiro Ueyama and Toshiya Tanaka rated the Japanese compositions. William Phillips and Brian Cullen rated the English compositions. Emiko Sugiura coded part of the protocol data. Keiko Shimazaki transcribed all the protocol data. Momomi Nakamura provided assistance at the proofreading stages. I am particularly grateful to Miyuki Sasaki, with whom I previously coauthored four papers related to the present study. Those previous studies not only helped me to sustain my interest in first and second language writing, but they also inspired me to pursue the present study myself. I am also indebted to William Phillips and Carol Rinnert for their insightful comments on earlier versions of several chapters. My special thanks go to Tanja Yoder, who gave editorial suggestions on earlier versions of the present volume with patience and kindness. Needless to say, the positions taken and any errors that may remain are solely my responsibility.

The overall study was planned when I was a research associate at Hiroshima University in 1996-1997. I deeply appreciate Professor Shogo Miura of Hiroshima University for his continuous encouragement during the years of the study. The data collection of Parts I and II was funded by a 1997 academic-year research grant from the President of Aichi Prefectural University. Furthermore, the data analysis was made possible by a Grant-in-Aid for Scientific Research (C)(2) (No. 12680281) from the Japan Society for the Promotion of Science for the academic years 2000-2002. The completion of the present research would have taken much more time without this generous support. Parts I and II of the present volume are an extensively revised version of the research report entitled "A preliminary study of writing strategies used by Japanese EFL students: For process-oriented English writing instruction," which was submitted to the Ministry of Education, Culture, Sports, Science, and Technology in 2003. Finally, the publication of the present volume was aided by a 2004 Grant-in-Aid for Scientific Research [Grant-in-Aid for Publication of Scientific Research Results] (No. 165170) from the Japan Society for the Promotion of Science.

Table of Contents

Acknowledgments   *v*

Introduction   *3*
   Background: English Writing Instruction in Japan   *3*
   The Present Study   *5*

Part I
Exploring Similarities and Differences in the Products of L1 (Japanese) and L2 (English) Writing

Chapter 1   L1 and L2 Organizational Patterns in the Argumentative Writing of Japanese EFL Students   *11*

   Previous Studies of Contrastive Rhetoric   *11*
      Japanese Rhetoric in Contrast to English Rhetoric   *11*
      Contrastive Rhetoric Research Dealing with Japanese L1 Writers   *15*
      Japanese Students' L1 and L2 Writing Background   *17*
      Recent Empirical Studies of English and Japanese Writing by the Same Writers   *21*

   Research Questions   *25*

   Method   *26*
      Participants   *26*
      Data   *28*
      Data Analysis   *32*

   Results and Discussion   *33*
      Research Question Set 1: Comparisons of L1 and L2 Organizational Patterns   *33*
      Research Question Set 2: Relations between Organizational Patterns and Composition Scores   *42*
      Research Question Set 3: Comparisons of L1 and L2 Organization-Planning Processes   *51*

Summary of Part I   *67*

Part II
Investigating L1 and L2 Writing Processes

Chapter 2   L1 and L2 Writing Processes of Low L2 Proficiency Level Students   *73*

Previous Studies of L1 and L2 Writing Processes   *73*

Research Questions   *78*

Method   *79*
    Participants   *79*
    Data   *79*
    Data Analysis   *81*

Results and Discussion   *82*
    L1 and L2 Writing Products   *82*
    L1 and L2 Writing Processes   *85*

Chapter 3   L1 and L2 Writing Processes of High L2 Proficiency Level Students   *100*

Research Questions   *101*

Method   *101*
    Participants   *101*

Results and Discussion   *102*
    L1 and L2 Writing Products   *102*
    L1 and L2 Writing Processes   *106*

Chapter 4   L1 and L2 Writing Processes: Low versus High L2 Proficiency Level Students   *122*

Results and Discussion   *122*
    L1 and L2 Writing Products   *122*
    L1 and L2 Writing Processes   *124*

Summary of Part II   *137*

Part III
Examining the Effects of L2 Writing Instruction on Student Writing

Chapter 5 Instruction on English Paragraph Organization *143*

English Paragraph Writing Instruction *144*

Research Questions *146*

Method *146*
- Participants *146*
- Content of Instruction on English Paragraphs *147*
- Data *148*
- Data Analysis *150*

Results and Discussion *150*
- *Research Question 1*: Comparisons of Pre- and Post-Instruction Compositions *150*
- *Research Question 2*: Comparisons of Pre- and Post-Instruction Compositions between the Two Writer Groups *153*
- *Research Question 3*: Students' Evaluations of Instructional Effects *160*

Chapter 6 Writing Strategies and Journal Writing Experience *170*

Journal Writing Experience *171*

Writing Strategy Instruction *172*

Research Questions *174*

Method *174*
- Participants *174*
- Content of Instruction *175*
- Data *179*
- Data Analysis *181*

Results and Discussion *181*
- *Research Question 1*: Comparisons of Pre- and Post-Instruction Compositions *181*
- *Research Question 2*: Comparisons of Pre- and Post-Instruction Writing Processes *184*
- *Research Question 3*: Characteristics of Writing Processes when Writing Improved *186*

Summary of Part III   *190*

Conclusion   *195*

Notes   *203*

References   *211*

Appendixes

    Appendix A: Macro-Level Organizational Patterns   *223*

    Appendix B: L1 and L2 Compositions Written by Ichiro (H)   *224*

    Appendix C: L1 and L2 Compositions Written by Hikari (H)   *226*

    Appendix D: L1 and L2 Compositions Written by Chihiro (L)   *228*

    Appendix E: L1 and L2 Compositions Written by Emi (L)   *230*

    Appendix F: Notes and Compositions Written by Ginko (H)   *232*

    Appendix G: Notes and Compositions Written by Beni (L)   *236*

    Appendix H: The Coding Categories of Introspective Reports during Pauses   *239*

    Appendix I: Postwriting Questionnaire   *243*

Product and Process in the L1 and L2 Writing of Japanese Students of English

Introduction

Background: English Writing Instruction in Japan

In Japan, students generally find it difficult to improve their English writing ability due to the paucity of writing practice in and out of the classroom. For example, English writing is not required for most Japanese students at university. English writing seems to be a minor focus in Japan. A large nation-wide survey conducted to examine university English teachers' views on English language education at mainly first- and second-year undergraduate levels found that 20% of the respondents did not engage in writing instruction at all (Koike et al., 1983). When writing was taught, further, the survey results showed that "structures and expressions" were most practiced (30.7%), followed by "translation from Japanese to English" (30.2%), "free composition" (17.0%), "others" (12.6%), and "reproduction, précis writing" (6.4%). English writing instruction, therefore, appears to be a service activity to reinforce the teaching of grammatical structures or vocabulary.

How do Japanese students perceive writing in English? Various questionnaire results have revealed Japanese university students' low level of motivation for writing English especially when compared with their high level of motivation for speaking English. Based on the results of a survey conducted at Hiroshima University, Igarashi, Inada, Iwamura, Fujimoto, and Yuasa (1976) interpreted the students' low expectations toward English writing courses as *"a blind spot of their motivation for*

English study" (my translation and my italics) (p. 12). According to probably the largest survey to date investigating Japanese university students' views of studying English, 61% of the students (N=10,095) wanted speaking instruction, whereas only 3.1% wanted writing instruction (Koike et al., 1985). This is not at all surprising given that students in Japan scarcely perceive immediate goals in terms of written English. The large-scale survey also reported that students provided the following responses when asked to choose among three alternative desirable goals of writing: (a) informal letters (61.9%), (b) writing required for future jobs (34.5%), and (c) academic papers (3.7%). For Japanese students, therefore, the most foreseeable goal of writing English is "informal letters." With the advancement of computer technology and the Internet, reports have begun to appear on correspondence in English via e-mail with students abroad (e.g., Suzuki, 1993). Thus, English writing may become more desirable and prevalent among Japanese, entailing a demand for such instruction as e-mail writing.

Although there are few Japanese university students (e.g., 3.7% of the students in Koike et al.'s 1985 survey) for whom academic writing in English is a foreseeable goal, at the graduate school level, students specializing not only in English-related subjects but also in science, technology, and engineering are nevertheless often required to write papers in English for their postgraduate degrees. For example, Gosden's (1996) Japanese doctoral students had writing a publishable scientific research article in English as a graduation requirement. In fact, English writing is an every-day experience for Japanese scientists, who have long perceived the need to do academic writing in English. This is illustrated by the fact that guidebooks and handbooks on how to write a paper in English are abundant for science-major students and researchers (e.g., Kinoshita, 1981). For example, *Nihon Butsuri Gakkai* (the Physical Society of

Japan) (1975; 1984) compiled essays by published writers in the field to promote better paper writing in English. Even with the availability of these books, it is not known how effective they are for those Japanese scientists who write papers in English.

The English language education field lacks L2 writing research that informs how Japanese students write in L2 and what types of L2 writing instruction they need to improve their L2 writing abilities. Much remains to be explored about how students write, how they learn to write, and what kinds of L2 writing instruction they require. By addressing these issues in the English as a Foreign Language (EFL) Japanese context, the present research should provide insights for both L2 writing research and teaching.

The Present Study

The present study deals with three strands of second language (L2) writing research: contrastive rhetoric, L2 writing processes in comparison with first language (L1) writing processes, and L2 writing pedagogy. The study is constituted of three major parts: (a) analysis of organizational patterns of students' L1/L2 writing, (b) analysis of students' L1/L2 writing processes, and (c) investigation of the effects of L2 writing instruction on student L2 writing. The present study is exploratory in nature and a precursor to a more confirmatory study with a larger sample size. Nevertheless, the study is characterized by the following innovative features: (a) it examines not only writing products but also writing processes of Japanese EFL university students; (b) it approaches contrastive rhetoric research from the point of view of writing processes; (c) it investigates the relationship between L1 and L2 writing using a within-subject design; (d) the participants for the first two parts consisted of two groups of Japanese EFL students with appropriate controls for L2 proficiency level and L2 instructional background; (e) the two groups' L1 and L2 writing processes were analyzed in terms of both intra- and inter-group comparisons; (f) teaching effects are examined for similar groups of EFL Japanese students empirically in the final part; (g) both quantified and qualified data are analyzed throughout the study.

Part I deals with organizational patterns of L1/L2 writing. The relationship between L1 and L2 writing has attracted the attention of L2 writing researchers. Despite the claim that Japanese rhetorical structures have organizational patterns distinct from English (e.g., Hinds, 1983), recent studies of contrastive rhetoric seem to cast doubts about such prevalent contentions (Kubota, 1992; McCagg, 1996). Recent studies have pointed to not only differences but also similarities between L1 and L2 writing. In Chapter 1, L1 (Japanese) and L2 (English) organizational patterns in the argumentative writing of Japanese students are compared. The present study makes within-subject comparisons of L1 and L2 compositions in terms of organizational patterns, organization scores, and overall quality.

The writing process analyses of the two groups are reported in Part II, which consists of Chapters 2, 3 and 4. Chapter 2 focuses on whether low L2 proficiency level students' L2 writing processes differ from those of L1, and Chapter 3 focuses on how high proficiency level

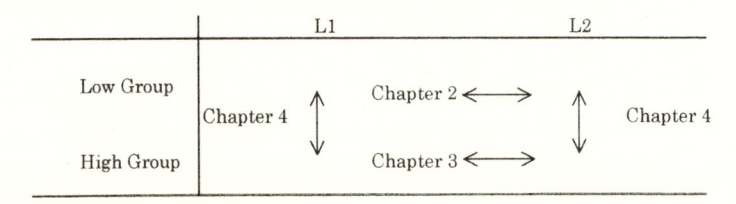

	L1		L2
Low Group	↑	Chapter 2 ←→	↑
	Chapter 4 ↕		↕ Chapter 4
High Group	↓	Chapter 3 ←→	↓

Figure 1: Comparisons Made in Part II of the Present Volume

students' L2 writing processes differ from those of L1. In Chapter 4, both L1 and L2 writing processes are compared respectively between the two groups. Figure 1 shows the comparisons the three chapters in Part II deal with.

Subsequently, Part III reports the effects of two types of L2 writing instruction on student writing. In Chapter 5, the effects of teaching about English paragraphs are examined. Then, in Chapter 6, writing strategy instruction with journal writing experience is implemented to investigate its effects on student writing.

Finally, in the Conclusion, the pedagogical implications of the study are drawn and directions for future studies are also discussed.

Part I

Exploring
Similarities and Differences
in the Products of L1 (Japanese)
and L2 (English) Writing

Chapter 1

L1 and L2 Organizational Patterns in the Argumentative Writing of Japanese EFL Students

Previous Studies of Contrastive Rhetoric

Japanese Rhetoric in Contrast to English Rhetoric

Based on his experience of correcting the English of papers Japanese physicists submitted to an academic physics journal, British physicist Anthony Leggett noticed common features in the English writing of Japanese physicists and wrote an essay addressed to them in 1966.[1] This essay seems to have been well read and even "very famous" [*Nihon Butsuri Gakkai* (Eds.), 1984, p. iv] in the physics field in Japan because it was reprinted in 1975 (Leggett, 1975), and later its Japanese translation appeared in 1984 (Leggett, 1984). Although it gives important insights into differences between Japanese and English writing, the essay is not well known outside the physics field and is thus worth introducing first in this chapter.

The five problems Leggett pointed out concerning Japanese English seem to be familiar ones in the contrastive rhetoric literature thereafter published. These five, which were actually presented in Japanese-English contrasts, are excerpted with original wording as follows:

1. In Japanese it seems that it is often legitimate to state a number of

thoughts in such a way that the connection between them, or the meaning of any given one, only becomes clear when one has read the whole paragraph or even the whole paper. This is not so in English; each sentence should be completely intelligible in the light only of what has *already* been written.

2. In English the sequence of thought should always be made quite explicit, even when, in Japanese, it would be legitimate to leave the reader to fill in the connection for himself.

3. In English it is essential to be precise and unambiguous. You may sometimes feel that it is advantageous to leave a certain amount of ambiguity in a statement, —a certain amount of 'room for manoeuvre' as it were; but this is never allowable in English.

4. Japanese seems to have a strong tendency to avoid too definite or assertive a statement, possibly because it is thought presumptuous to impose one's own views on the reader without conceding that there are possible alternatives.

5. To an English reader, Japanese (and J.E.) often seems vague and diffuse—there seem to be many clauses or sentences which add nothing substantial to the meaning. In English, on the contrary, every clause should 'pull its weight'. (Leggett, 1966, pp. 791-792)

Coincidentally, in the same year 1966, American applied linguist Robert Kaplan published a pioneering work of contrastive rhetoric, in which he analyzed the organization of English paragraphs written by five different L1 groups of English as a Second Language (ESL) students (Kaplan, 1966). Of the five types (see Figure 2 below), a typical paragraph organization of Asian languages, although Japanese was not included in his analysis, was characterized as "turning and turning in a widening gyre" (p. 10).[2] That is, Chinese and Korean writers were described as being circular

English   Semitic   Oriental   Romance   Russian

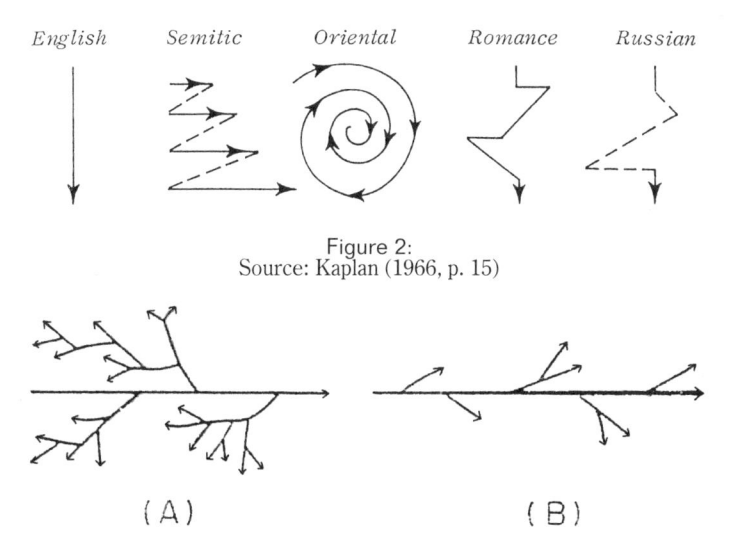

Figure 2:
Source: Kaplan (1966, p. 15)

(A)   (B)

Figure 3:
adapted from Leggett (1966, p. 791)

and getting to the point only at the end. This is related to the first and fifth points Leggett (1966) made regarding Japanese writing. In contrast, the writing of native English speakers was shown to follow a straight-line linear development. As for the other three language groups' patterns, Kaplan's (1966) diagram of five different paragraph organizations has been widely reprinted and discussed. As the figure shows, the Asian pattern is depicted as a converging circle. Interestingly, Leggett (1966) also attempted to contrast English-Japanese patterns as diagramed in Figure 3, "where the 'direction of reading' is from left to right" (Leggett 1966, p. 791). According to his explanation, (A) illustrates the Japanese pattern in the eyes of an English reader, whereas (B) shows the only allowable pattern in English. The Japanese pattern has many diverging digressions in a backward direction, whereas the English counterpart has far fewer digressions and these are all in a forward direction (arrows were added for visual clarity). Although Leggett's (1966) diagram is not widely known or quoted in the contrastive rhetoric field, his instinctive characterizations of Japanese versus English can be considered a pioneering work about the Japanese-English contrastive rhetoric.

Kaplan's study (1966) initiated many follow-up contrastive rhetoric studies. Such studies that included Japanese writing were notably Hinds (1983; 1987; 1990). Hinds (1987), in particular, asserted that Japanese is a "reader-responsible" language that places responsibility on the reader for successful communication in contrast to "writer-responsible" English. The reader-responsible aspect of Japanese is similar to Leggett's (1966) second point above. Related to Hinds' (1987) writer-versus-reader responsibility distinction, Okabe (1983) used a "line" versus "point/dot/space" contrast to depict a difference in communication patterns between the United States and Japan. In connection with this point-/dot-/space-like communication in Japanese, Loveday (1983) pointed out that "one of the characteristic patterns of Japanese oral and written discourse is the dot-type presentation of one item after the other in a highly anecdotal or episodic vein without articulating the conclusion" (p. 185). Furthermore, Okabe (1983) attributed the difference in communication patterns to compositions of respective societies. According to Okabe (1983), because little is taken for granted in a heterogeneous U.S. society, everything must be spelled out and be precise with no need to fill in gaps. On the other hand, in a relatively homogeneous Japanese society, everything should not necessarily be spelled out explicitly because much is already shared, which enables the listener/reader to fill in information even in a stepping-stone type of communication. In other words, Japanese does not have to be precise and unambiguous like English (i.e., Leggett's third point).

Another dichotomy of Japanese and English rhetorics is in

Americans' preference for "primacy and anticlimactic principles of organization" versus the Japanese reliance on "recency and climactic principles" (Okabe, 1983, p. 30). Furthermore, Naotsuka (1980) claimed that the Japanese tendency to preserve the most important point until the end without first giving a bird's-eye picture was likely to cause misunderstanding in communication with Europeans and Americans who tend to state the conclusion first. Related to Leggett's fourth point above, it has also been argued that Japanese tend to be reluctant to express personal opinions explicitly, tending instead to be indirect in expression (e.g., Naotsuka & Sakamoto et al., 1981).

These characteristics of Japanese organization patterns or rhetoric in contrast to English counterparts are prevalent in books and articles in Japan, and Japanese students are relatively familiar with them (e.g., Kubota, 1992). They have been influential characterizations not only in contrastive rhetoric research but also in L1/L2 writing pedagogy (e.g., Kinoshita, 1981; 1990); but they have remained to be verified by empirical studies.

Contrastive Rhetoric Research Dealing with Japanese L1 Writers

Those contrasting features between Japanese and English are claimed to make L1 Japanese writers' L2 English difficult to follow, especially for non-L1 Japanese readers or listeners who do not share similar rhetorical backgrounds. When L1 Japanese writers write in L2, they are believed to transfer their L1 features to L2. Contrastive rhetoric research was such a field that examined problems encountered by L2 writers and attempted to explain them with reference to their L1. It has now expanded its scope to encompass not only organizational patterns but also writing processes involved (Connor, 1996; Matsuda, 1997).

Previous contrastive rhetoric research involving Japanese writers has found mixed results concerning organization. On the one hand, Japanese is claimed to have organizational patterns distinct from English (e.g., Hinds, 1983, 1990). On the other hand, some studies cast doubts on such claims (Kubota, 1992, 1998b). Is there any characteristic of text organization specific to Japanese writing? It is often argued that in opinion-stating essays Japanese writers are hesitant to take a position initially, and the reader has to wait for the writer to state his/her position until the final part of the text (e.g., Oi, 1986). This tendency to postpone one's main point until a later position has been found not only in student texts but also in those written by professional writers. Based on his analysis of the column *tensei jingo* (*Vox Populi, Vox Dei*) from the *Asahi Shimbun*, one of the major Japanese newspapers, Hinds (1990) characterized the Japanese organizational pattern as "quasi-inductive." Similarly, Maynard (1996) analyzed 38 opinion columns from the same newspaper, and suggested that Japanese is "bottom-heavy" in the sense of sentence, paragraph, and the whole text. Reviewing the findings of contrastive rhetoric studies on English and Japanese, Kubota (1998a) concluded, "one feature commonly identified by researchers as a characteristic of Japanese writing is 'induction' " (p. 478).

Such a "bottom-heavy" tendency has been also observed in L2 English texts written by Japanese learners of English. Contrastive rhetoric studies have found that Japanese EFL students tend to employ the specific-to-general (inductive) organization, whereas American L1 students are more inclined to use the general-to-specific (deductive) organization in English (e.g., Kobayashi, 1984; Oi, 1984). However, deductive patterns were also reported to be employed by L2 Japanese writers. Kobayashi (1984) found many Japanese EFL university students used the specific-to-general organizational pattern, whereas advanced Japanese

ESL students studying in the U.S. tended to favor the general-to-specific pattern. Oi (1984) also found that just over half of the Japanese EFL students writing in L2 had a preference for the general-to-specific organization, whereas American university students overall showed a stronger preference for this pattern. Drawing on 130 English expository compositions written by intermediate and advanced Japanese students in the U.S., Achiba and Kuromiya (1983) discovered that linear (deductive) rhetorical patterns (34%) were most frequently employed, followed by circular and inductive patterns (27%). These previous studies suggest that L2 Japanese students with some L2 writing experience or a certain English proficiency level may tend to use the organizational pattern that many studies have identified as the preferred L1 English one.

The transfer of organizational patterns from L1 to L2 has been a controversial issue. Some argue that L2 organization reflects that of L1, whereas others claim that poor L2 organization manifests only a developmental problem rather than L1 transfer (Mohan & Lo, 1985). We cannot discuss student L2 organizational patterns without taking into consideration student L1 and L2 writing backgrounds in terms of writing conventions, instruction, and experience, as well as L2 proficiency level. L1 writing instruction Japanese students have received is found to exert inevitable influences on their L2 writing (e.g., Kobayashi & Rinnert, 2002). Thus, in this chapter Japanese students' writing background is considered before a review of previous findings on the L1/L2 writing relationship.

Japanese Students' L1 and L2 Writing Background

Regarding L1 writing conventions, the *ki-shô-ten-ketsu* pattern has often been used to characterize Japanese writing. According to this pattern, the writer introduces the topic in *ki*, develops the topic in *shô*, then makes a transition in *ten*, and finally concludes the topic in *ketsu*. Most Japanese are familiar with this writing pattern. However, there is no definitive interpretation of the pattern (Kubota, 1998a). It was originally derived from a Chinese poetry form, and some claim the pattern should be restricted to literary writing, because it is most appropriate for writing that attempts to move or appeal emotionally to readers (e.g., Kinoshita, 1990). Nevertheless, this organizational pattern can be applied to many genres of writing. In argumentative writing, for example, the writer states his/her position (*ki*), gives supporting reasons for the position (*shô*), introduces a counterargument and opposes it with further reasons (*ten*), and restates the position (*ketsu*). This use of the *ki-shô-ten-ketsu* in argumentative writing is actually exemplified in high school Japanese writing textbooks (e.g., Ôoka, et al., 1998). Of the four sections, the *ten*, which is believed to make an abrupt transition in the development of the argument, has attracted the most attention (e.g., Hinds, 1983), because it is considered alien to English organizational patterns. However, the *ten* section in argumentative writing can be regarded as a development of the discussion from a different viewpoint from that of the writer to further justify his/her position. In this light, the transition may not be alien but even acceptable to L1 English readers. This view of the *ki-shô-ten-ketsu* pattern may indicate the possibility of similar rhetorical structures in argumentative writing between Japanese and English, although this certainly requires further investigation.

In regard to L1 writing instruction, Japanese students do not generally receive any formal L1 expository or academic writing instruction at any level of Japanese education. They have the most writing experience in expressive writing (writing about their experiences in journals/diaries), summaries and *kansôbun* (personal impressions) of materials read, and the least in expository and argumentative writing at school (e.g.,

JACET Kansai Chapter Writing Teaching Group, 1995). The traditional view of Japanese writing instruction has attached great importance to writing about what the writer hears, sees, thinks or feels, which inspires emotion in the readers (Ôkuma, 1997).[3] Japanese students are generally accustomed to writing about their personal experience and feelings in L1 (Murai, 1990). Writing about one's personal thinking or feeling directly on paper seems to have constituted the basis of L1 Japanese composition instruction. According to this view of writing, the important point is whether the reader empathizes with the writer when reading the text. This view still has a great influence on Japanese writing instruction, but many writing researchers/practitioners have realized this type of writing is not sufficient, and that it is also necessary for Japanese students to learn expository writing (e.g., Kinoshita 1981; Ôkuma, 1997). For example, based on his experience as a reviewer for an international journal of physics, Kinoshita (1981) noticed that many of the Japanese authors submitting manuscripts lacked the kind of rhetorical and expository writing instruction that has been provided in the United States and he advocated the implementation of such writing instruction in Japan.[4]

In spite of such perceptions suggesting the necessity for instruction, L1 writing courses are not usually offered even at universities, which is in sharp contrast with U.S. universities (Connor, 1996). For example, as a Japanese who was born and received education up to graduate school level in Japan, I did not take a single L1 writing course, and other Japanese bilingual academics share this background (see Casanave, 1998). L1 academic writing tends to be self-taught, and it is taken for granted that students are able to write an academic paper for a course they take at university. Although expository/argumentative writing instruction rarely has a place in the Japanese educational system, some high school students may receive preparatory lessons geared for *shôronbun*, which in English literally means a short thesis or essay but refers to specific writing for examination purposes. Many universities require *shôronbun* as part of the entrance examination. In *shôronbun*, writers are supposed to state their thoughts (opinions, interpretations) based on analysis and/or synthesis of facts regarding a given topic (Kabashima, Uegaki, Soda, & Satake, 1989). In a typical *shôronbun*, students read a Japanese passage and write expository prose concerning the thesis of the passage or issues provided by the passage. The past *shôronbun* questions are available to the public through publications of preparatory schools (e.g., Kawaijuku Shôronbunka, 2002), so examination candidates can prepare using similar tasks before taking the entrance examinations. Some high schools offer supplementary lessons for *shôronbun* writing. Even without being given such preparatory courses at school, students can take such lessons in a commercial examination preparatory school, and some may also receive individual instruction through correspondence courses. They can also resort to handbooks and guidebooks on how to produce good *shôronbun*. Although students' experiences with *shôronbun* instruction vary from null to extensive, we cannot ignore its possible effects on student writing. At university, students take written tests or write research reports/papers in L1, or both, for their course evaluations.[5]

Regarding L2 English writing, Japanese student experience is practically non-existent. L2 writing instruction in high school is oriented toward translation from L1 to L2 at the sentence level (e.g., JACET Kansai Chapter Writing Teaching Group, 1995). According to Koike et al. (1983), translation at the sentence level is one of the most common writing practices not only in high schools but also in universities in Japan. Instead of having had English writing experience beyond a sentence level, Japanese students have been taught to be more concerned with grammatical accuracy at the sentence level.

Because writing is the least emphasized skill in English language education at every level including university, it is possible for a Japanese non-English major university graduate not to have taken any English writing courses or not to have had any English writing experience. In such cases, it can be assumed that L1 writing instruction/experience predominantly influences how students write in L2. Examining Arabic and Japanese ESL students' L1 writing backgrounds, Liebman (1992) found that the Japanese regarded persuasive writing to be like expressive writing in that writers express their personal emotions, which was in sharp contrast with the Arabic students who considered logic or supporting evidence essential to persuasive writing. The differences found in their perceptions of persuasive writing can be partly explained by their previous L1 writing backgrounds. The Japanese students in Liebman's (1992) study had reportedly received expressive writing instruction using journals, whereas the Arabic students received transactional writing instruction including discussion and peer reading. Without much argumentative writing experience in L1, EFL Japanese university students can therefore be expected to have problems with argumentative writing in L2. Inexperience with such writing in L1, not to mention unfamiliarity with L2 writing, may cause problems in L2 argumentative writing, which result from "both developmental and transfer factors" (Mohan & Lo, 1985, p. 517).

Recent Empirical Studies of English and Japanese Writing by the Same Writers

While early empirical studies of English-Japanese contrastive rhetoric used between-group comparisons (e.g., Kobayashi, 1984; Oi, 1984), several later studies have investigated Japanese students' L1 and L2 texts using a within-subject research design. As has been argued, it is risky and difficult, if not impossible, to generalize preferred rhetorical patterns of a language based on a small sample size of texts. It is even more complicated to account for rhetorical patterns used by L2 writers. L2 texts reflect various entangled factors that include not only writers' L2 writing ability, proficiency, and writing experience, but also L1 factors such as their writing ability, instructional background, and writing experience. These multi-faceted aspects of L2 writing call for studies that can explore relations between L1 and L2 texts for each individual student. As Kubota (1998b) pointed out, contrastive rhetoric research should investigate L1-L2 transfer in writing as a within-subject phenomenon. Although still small in number, these within-subject studies constitute an important step in exploring how an individual student organizes L1/L2 texts and whether each student's L1/L2 organizations are similar. Whereas previous contrastive rhetoric studies involving Japanese and English had a tendency to focus on differences (see Connor, 1996, for a review), these recent studies shed light on similarities between them.

To date several studies have investigated the relationship between L1 and L2 texts using a within-subject design. For example, Kamimura (1996), Sasaki and Hirose (1996) and Kubota (1998b) examined L1 (Japanese) and L2 (English) writing by EFL Japanese university students. Kamimura (1996) found positive correlations between L1 and L2 narrative compositions, especially among those written by students with a high L2 proficiency level. Similarly, Sasaki and Hirose (1996) found significant positive correlations between total scores of L1 and L2 argumentative compositions.[6] Using a retrospective questionnaire to explore writing processes, they also revealed that the good writers were concerned with overall organization both before and while writing in L1 and L2. In fact, attention to organization was the only writing strategy found to be significantly different from the weak writers. Examining Japanese university students' L1 and L2 expository and persuasive writing from the perspective of organization, Kubota (1998b) revealed that (a) L1 and L2 texts had similarities in organization, (b) L1 and L2 organization scores correlated positively in both types of texts and (c) students with limited L2 proficiency lacked attention to organization. Although Kubota's (1998b) participants' L2 proficiency levels were not reported, they were third- and fourth-year university undergraduates and graduates who were assumed to "reflect the outcome of academic training in Japan" (p. 76). Using a similar method to analyze L1/L2 organizational patterns within the writing of each individual student, Hirose (2003c) found that in L2, Japanese EFL student-writers chose deductive organizational patterns, whereas in L1, they chose either deductive or inductive patterns, although those choosing the latter were much smaller in number. The finding that most students used deductive organizations for both L1 and L2 did not concur with the findings of earlier research (e.g., Kobayashi, 1984).

Although these results should be treated with caution because of the small sample sizes, these recent studies suggest that similarities in L1/L2 organizational patterns may deserve more attention. These recent contrastive rhetoric studies appear to suggest that the good Japanese EFL students write in L2 not so differently from L1 in terms of organization, whereas weak students do not pay attention to organization. Nevertheless, the relations of student L2 proficiency levels to their use of organizational patterns have not been fully examined yet and are still inconclusive.

Furthermore, the relation between choice of organizational patterns and text evaluation is another inconclusive issue that requires further research. For example, Kubota (1998b) reported that Japanese L1 texts with inductive organization were likely to receive lower evaluations by experienced Japanese readers, suggesting that deductive organization may be as highly valued in Japanese as in English. On the other hand, Hirose (2003c) found that L1 compositions with inductive organization received neither higher nor lower evaluations from experienced L1 raters than those with deductive organization. That is, differences in the choice of rhetorical patterns did not seem to have had much influence on the organization score nor on the total score. Thus, Kubota (1998b) and Hirose (2003c) reported apparently opposing results concerning evaluations of L1 Japanese rhetorical organization.

Related to this evaluation, Japanese students' own perceived preferences regarding rhetorical patterns have not also been fully addressed except in a few recent studies such as Kubota (1998b) and Rinnert and Kobayashi (2001). Kubota (1998b) found Japanese students tended to organize texts inductively, whereas, on reflection, they showed their preference for the deductive style. Furthermore, Rinnert and Kobayashi (2001) showed that the more L2 writing experience EFL learners, including teachers, have had, the closer their perceptions of English writing come to those of L1 English native speakers (= teachers). Student perceptions of L1/L2 writing are presumably influenced by not only the L1/L2 instruction they have received at school, but also the information available through mass media, such as books and magazines. The dichotomy between "direct English" and "indirect Japanese" expression is a prevalent stereotype among Japanese students (see Hirose, 2001, and Silva, 1992, for similar views from Japanese students). What are Japanese students' preferred organizational patterns in Japanese and English? Are their preferred patterns in the two languages similar? These issues require empirical investigation based on students' own L1/L2 writing.

Thus, we are in need of studies that investigate not only rhetorical organizations of L1/L2 texts but also their relation to student L2 proficiency level and text evaluation, by controlling student L2 proficiency levels. As a follow-up study to Hirose (2003c), the present study examined student L1/L2 argumentative writing, which has not been studied until recently in contrastive rhetoric studies (Connor, 1996). Furthermore, the present study also took writing processes into consideration to examine fully how and why students use certain rhetorical patterns in L1/L2. More specifically, processes involved in planning organization were examined, and the process analysis complemented the product analysis. The present study is similar to Henry (1993), who analyzed 5 mature ESL students' processes of making rhetorical choices, in that contrastive rhetoric research is done taking writing processes into consideration.[7]

Research Questions

The present chapter investigates the relationship between Japanese students' L1 and L2 writing in terms of writing products, especially organization. The study addressed the following three sets of research questions:

1. Are there differences in organizational patterns between L1 and L2 argumentative texts written by the same Japanese EFL students? Is there any relation between student L2 proficiency level and L2 organizational patterns?
2. Are there differences in L1/L2 organization and overall quality of the argumentative texts written by the same Japanese EFL students? Are they different depending on student L2 proficiency level? What is the relation between organizational patterns and evaluation in L1/L2

argumentative texts?

3. How are the L1 and L2 organization-planning processes different within each individual student? Are they different depending on student L2 proficiency level?

Method

Participants

A total of 11 Japanese university students (5 men and 6 women) participated in the present study. The participants took the Comprehensive English Language Test (CELT) Form A (Harris & Palmer, 1986). Volunteers were solicited from among students in three classes based on their CELT scores (see the Participants sections in Chapters 2 and 3 for details), and they were financially compensated for their work. Table 1 presents the means, SDs, and ranges of the CELT scores per group. The high group consisted of 5 third-year students majoring in British and

Table 1: Descriptive Statistics of Participants' CELT Scores (N=11)

Measure (total possible)	Low (n=5) M	SD	Range	High (n=6) M	SD	Range
CELT Listening (100)	38.4	8.4	30-52	82.0	10.6	64-92
CELT Structure (100)	54.8	5.9	49-64	88.7	4.9	80-93
CELT Vocabulary (100)	34.6	8.4	24-44	69.7	7.0	63-81
CELT Total (300)	127.8	11.8	110-142	240.3	14.3	216-260

Notes: Low Group (M=2, F=3) Mean Age=18.6
High Group (M=3, F=3) Mean Age=21.2

American Studies and 1 graduate student specializing in English language education, and the low group was constituted of 5 first-year students whose major was British and American Studies at a night school. The results of Mann-Whitney U, a nonparametric test for comparisons between two groups, found significant differences between the two groups in every aspect of CELT: structure, listening, vocabulary and total score. Thus, the L2 proficiency level of the high group was significantly higher than that of the low group.

The two groups were different not only in L2 proficiency level but also in instructional background in L2 writing. The high group had taken several university-level English composition classes for at least a year and had some writing experience, whereas the low group had not taken the classes yet and scarcely had any L2 writing experience before. The five high-group students who were third-year students all took a course in the basics of academic writing when they were in their second year. The course focused on organizing and developing essays with particular attention given to logical and appropriate language use for academic writing. English native-speaking professors were in charge of these writing courses, and students learned the key concepts of formal writing such as topic sentence and the three-part structure of introduction, body, and conclusion, and had written expository essays. The ultimate goal of these writing courses was to prepare students to develop academic writing skills necessary to write a research paper in English. The fact that high group students all had some formal writing experience in English is important because Japanese EFL students, like the low group students in the present study, often lack such experience, and whether they have writing experience or not has been found to influence writing quality (Kubota, 1998b; Sasaki & Hirose, 1996). Thus, students' L2 proficiency level paralleled their L2 writing experience: The higher their level of L2 proficiency, the more L2 writing experience they had. These two groups can be termed as "novice" or "inexperienced" and "experienced" EFL writer groups. In the present study, however, the names "low" and "high" English proficiency groups are used, respectively, for simplicity.

Data

(1) L1 and L2 Compositions

An argumentative task requiring the writer to take one of two positions and supporting that position was chosen for both L1 and L2. Argumentative writing was used in the present study because it was considered appropriate to examine whether the high-proficiency group with an L2 writing instructional background and the low-proficiency group without such a background differ in their organizational patterns of L1/L2 compositions.[8] The task of taking one position and arguing for the position may be considered "problematic for L2 writers from more interdependently oriented cultural backgrounds" (Ramanathan & Atkinson, 1999, p. 61) such as Japanese. Past studies that dealt with Japanese EFL students have used similar tasks but without reporting the participants' problems with this type of argumentative task (e.g., Hirose 2003c; Sasaki & Hirose, 1996).

Different topics were used to avoid the possible influence of participants' first writing on the second writing because L1/L2 data were collected from each participant with a short interval on the same day. The topics were considered relatively familiar to the students, because they were expected to have personal experience related to the topics. In order to avoid a possible order effect, L1/L2 tasks were counterbalanced. Five participants from the two groups first wrote in L2, and then in L1, after a break, and the remaining 6 wrote in the opposite order (L1→L2). The participants were not informed beforehand that they would be writing, nor about the topics. They were asked to write for 30 minutes, but they were allowed to stop when, or continue until, they felt they had finished.[9] They did not use a dictionary.[10]

The following prompts were given in L1:

L1: In the readers' column in a Japanese newspaper, there has been a heated discussion about the custom of "non-Christian Japanese celebrating Christmas" by holding parties or exchanging presents. Some people think it is a good custom, whereas others believe it should be abolished. Now the editor of the newspaper is calling for the readers' opinions. Suppose you are writing for the readers' opinion column. Take one of the positions described above, and write your opinion in Japanese.

L2: In the readers' column in an English newspaper, there has been a heated discussion about the issue of "school uniforms." Some people think that high school students should wear school uniforms, whereas others believe students should choose what to wear at school. Now the editor of the newspaper is calling for the readers' opinions. Suppose you are writing for the readers' opinion column. Take one of the positions described above, and write your opinion in English.

Different rating scales were used to measure participants' L1 and L2 writing abilities because readers' expectations may be different in evaluating L1 Japanese and L2 English compositions. The L2 compositions were scored by two native-speaker English professors who taught English writing courses at Japanese universities. Following

Jacobs, Zinkgraf, Wormuth, Hartfiel and Hughey's (1981) ESL Composition Profile, ratings were assigned for the five differently weighted criteria: <u>content</u>, <u>organization</u>, <u>vocabulary</u>, <u>language use</u>, and <u>mechanics</u> (see Table 3). According to Hamp-Lyons (1990), the Profile is "the best-known scoring procedure for ESL writing at the present time" (p. 78). Each participant's L2 score was the sum of the two raters' scores, with a possible range of 68 to 200 points. Similarly, the L1 compositions were rated by three Japanese professors who were researchers specialized in L1 Japanese language education. Using the L1 rating scale specifically developed for this type of L1 Japanese writing (Sasaki & Hirose, 1999), six criteria were employed, each receiving 30 points; <u>clarity of the theme</u>, <u>appeal to the readers</u>, <u>expression</u>, <u>organization</u>, <u>knowledge of language forms</u>, and <u>social awareness</u> (see Table 4). Each participant's L1 score was the sum of the three raters' scores, with a possible range of 18 to 180 points.[11] All the raters in the present study scored the compositions individually without a practice session, which was not possible to arrange because of practical constraints.

(2) Analysis of L1 and L2 Organizational Patterns

In order to examine English and Japanese organizational patterns, the present study applied the three types of analysis originally employed by Kubota's (1992) comparative study: (a) the location of main idea(s), (b) the macro-level rhetorical pattern, and (c) presence or absence of a summary statement.[12] Some categories were simplified for the present study (see Kubota, 1992, for a complete list).[13] In this study, a main idea was considered as a writer's opinion-stating sentence. First, the location of the sentence was identified as one of the following four: (a) <u>Initial</u> (stated in the introduction), (b) <u>Middle</u> (in the middle section), (c) <u>Final</u> (in the conclusion), or (d) <u>Obscure</u> (not clearly stated). There were no cases of more than one position taken in the same text. For each text, the macro-level rhetorical pattern was identified as one of the following three major patterns: (a) Explanation (the writer's opinion precedes a supporting reason), (b) Specification (the writer's opinion and a preview statement of a supporting reason are followed by the reason), or (c) Induction (a supporting reason precedes the writer's opinion) (see Appendix A for more detailed categorization). The Explanation and Specification were considered instances of deductive style, whereas Induction was regarded as inductive style. Thirdly, the presence or absence of a summary statement at the end of the text was coded as one of the following three: (a) + (the writer's opinion on the topic is re-presented or what was discussed in the text is summarized), (b) − (neither opinion nor summary is presented), or (c) 0 (the writer's opinion is located at the end of the essay).

(3) L1 and L2 Organization-Planning Processes

I collected the process data individually. The whole data collection process took approximately two hours per participant. The data collection procedure was adapted from that of Anzai and Uchida (1981). Participants were videotaped from the time they were handed a task sheet up until they finished the work. Immediately after they started writing, they were interrupted and interviewed about the first sentence they had just begun to write; in particular, they were asked whether they had planned what to write in the conclusion and in the middle section. Immediately after they finished writing, I also asked them follow-up questions in order to check the validity of their initial interview responses, that is, to examine the extent to which their planning at the time of writing the first word actually matched their writing. This part of the protocol data, in addition to the verbal reports made immediately after they started writing the first word, was mainly used for the analysis reported in the present chapter.

The participants then watched the video that showed them writing and they responded to my questions about what they were doing during pauses. This part of the protocol data is not used for the present chapter except for the portions where they made comments on the organization of their texts. The students' retrospective reports of what they were doing during pauses are used for the analysis reported in Chapters 2, 3, and 4. All the interviews, conducted in L1, were audiotaped and transcribed for analysis. All the quotes from oral interview exchanges in the present study are my translations.

Data Analysis

For *Research Question Set 1*, the L1/L2 compositions of the participants were compared in terms of the three points mentioned above. An experienced Japanese EFL teacher who was independent of the present study and I did the coding. There was 95.5% agreement for the location of the opinion-statement sentence, 81.8% for the macro-level rhetorical pattern, and 100% for the summary statement. In the case of discrepancies, we arrived at an agreement on them after discussion. However, in one case of disagreement concerning the location of an opinion-stating sentence, we resorted to a third rater, a researcher specialized in L2 writing, and reported the coding that two of the three raters agreed on.

For *Research Question Set 2*, the L1/L2 compositions were compared in terms of organization and total scores. The Wilcoxon Matched-Pairs Signed-Ranks test, a nonparametric equivalent of the paired *t*-test, was conducted to check for statistically significant differences. Because the sample size of the present study was not large, applying parametric procedures to the results was not considered appropriate. Because I made two comparisons, organization and total scores, the alpha level of 0.05 for the study was adjusted to 0.025 by a Bonferroni correction for multiple comparison (Tabachnick & Fidell, 1996). Furthermore, correlations among total and subscores of L1/L2 compositions were all measured. The overall length of L1/L2 compositions was also measured by counting the total number of characters/words per composition. Furthermore, the Mann-Whitney U tests were conducted to check for statistically significant differences between the two groups in the total scores and subscores of L1/L2 compositions. Because I made 6 comparisons for L2 composition scores, 5 subscores and total score, the alpha level of 0.05 was adjusted to 0.0083 by a Bonferroni correction for multiple comparison. For L1 composition scores, I made 7 comparisons, 6 subscores and total score, and the alpha level of 0.05 was adjusted to 0.007 by a Bonferroni correction.

For *Research Question Set 3*, the person who rated L1/L2 organizational patterns and I analyzed the student process data (transcribed data) separately to grasp what students planned before writing, what they thought of their own texts compared with their initial planning, and what, if anything, they said about their rhetorical choices in the follow-up interviews. We summarized the findings together.

Results and Discussion

Research Question Set 1: Comparisons of L1 and L2 Organizational Patterns

(1) Overall Organizational Patterns

Table 2 presents the results of the two coders' analysis of the organizational patterns of students' compositions. All participant names are pseudonyms in the present study. The low group students were given names starting from A to E (Aya, Beni, Chihiro, Dan, and Emi), whereas high group students had names that started with F to K (Fumi, Ginko, Hikari, Ichiro, Jiro, and Ken). Chihiro and Dan in the low group were male, and so were Ichiro, Jiro, and Ken in the high group.

Table 2: Location of Main Ideas, Macro-Level Patterns, and Summary Statements

	Main Idea		Macro-Level Pattern		Summary Statement	
Writer (Group)	L1	L2	L1	L2	L1	L2
Aya (Low)	Initial	Initial	Explanation (Comparison)	Explanation (Collection)	−	−
Beni (Low)	Initial	Initial	Explanation (Collection)	Explanation (Collection)	−	−
Chihiro (Low)	Final	Obscure	Other	Other	0	−
Dan (Low)	Initial	Initial	Explanation (Collection)	Explanation (Collection)	+	+
Emi (Low)	Middle	Middle	Explanation (Collection)	Explanation (Collection)	+	−
Fumi (High)	Initial	Initial	Explanation (Collection)	Explanation (Collection)	+	−
Ginko (High)	Initial	Initial	Explanation (Collection)	Explanation (Comparison)	+	+
Hikari (High)	Final	Initial	Induction (Collection)	Specification (Collection)	0	−
Ichiro (High)	Initial	Initial	Specification (Comparison)	Explanation (Collection)	+	−
Jiro (High)	Final	Initial	Induction	Explanation (Collection)	0	+
Ken (High)	Final	Initial	Other	Explanation (Collection)	0	+

Regarding the location of main idea, in L2, 9 out of 11 participants (81.8%) put their positions in the initial section. In L1, however, 6 participants (54.5%) stated their positions in the initial section, 4 (36.4%) in the final section, and 1 (9%) in the middle section. As Table 2 shows, the results of macro-level rhetorical pattern analysis revealed that in L2 all participants, except one low student, chose deductive organizational patterns (i.e., position-statement preceding a number of reasons, exemplified as either Explanation or Specification). No students of the present study employed inductive style in L2, which is often claimed to characterize texts written by Japanese students (e.g., Kobayashi, 1984; Oi, 1984). Like the location of the main idea, L1 texts showed more variation in macro-level pattern. Regarding the presence or absence of a summary statement, the presence was more conspicuous in L1. If opinion statements at the end of the text (coded as 0) were also included in the total number present, 9 students (81.8%) finished with a position statement/restatement or summary statement. In contrast, in L2, only 4 students (36.4%) provided such endings.

On the whole, the students showed their preference for initial positioning of their main idea, deductive type organization, and to a lesser extent the absence of a summary statement in L2. In L1, their preferences were divided in terms of the positioning of their main idea and the use of macro-level patterns, whereas they all clearly showed a preference for the presence of a summary statement. These results implied that there were some differences between L1 and L2 organizational patterns. Overall, the results of organizational patterns did not support the view that Japanese prefer an inductive style (e.g., Kubota, 1998a).

The results of the analysis of location of main idea, macro-level patterns, and summary statement are each discussed separately below.

(2) Location of Main Idea

The participants' overall tendency to state their positions initially in L2 and, to a lesser degree in L1, seems not to conform to the following discourse features pointed out as typical of Japanese writing: "overall organization moving from specific to general," "no strong specific position taken by the writer, thus leaving more up to the reader" and "presentation of the topic in the introduction without indicating a specific point of view about it" (Rinnert & Kobayashi, 2001, p. 192). Oi (1986) also reported that Japanese students "usually start with hesitation or [a] neutral statement; they wait until the last part of [the] text to reveal their stance" (p. 44). Most students in the present study showed no hesitation to reveal their stance initially. It is particularly noteworthy that they showed no hesitancy in L2. This result suggests that deductive patterns may not be difficult for Japanese students to learn to employ especially in their L2 writing, and instruction can be effective in this respect.

    The present results concerning the positioning of the main point can be derived from the opinion letter task itself. The explicit task of taking a position on an issue may have pushed them to express their positions for/against the given topic at the outset of their writing, and influenced their choice of organizational patterns. Nevertheless, the main idea does not always appear at the outset of the introductory paragraph in English. According to Rinnert and Kobayashi (2001), the introductory paragraph of English essays "tend[s] to contain a thesis statement toward or at the end of the introduction" (p. 201) rather than at the beginning of the paragraph. The organization of such writing can be expected to differ from those of the readers' opinion columns in a newspaper. For example, opinion letters often begin with an identification of the article or the issue being responded to and a writer's agreement/disagreement or the evaluation of the article. Furthermore, the topic of the opinion letter may have also affected the writer's choice of the organization of text (A. Kirkpatrick, personal communication, July 1, 2003). The topics used in the present study were relatively safe in that the writer could present his/her position straightforwardly. That is, the school uniforms and Japanese custom of celebrating Christmas topics are easier to state one's position than a currently controversial topic, for example, about dispatching Japanese Self-Defense Forces to Iraq, especially when the writer's opinion differs from that of the Japanese government or the general public. Furthermore, there is the possibility that how the writer perceives his/her relationship with the reader also affects the writer's choice of organizational patterns. As pointed out by Kirkpatrick (1997), the organizational patterns of text can be decided by the relative power relationship between the writer and the reader.[14] Given the same topic, therefore, the organization may be different depending on the relationship. More specifically, the organization of the letter to the readers' opinion column is likely to differ from that of a letter addressed to the Prime Minister, for example.

(3) Macro-Level Rhetorical Pattern

Regardless of language, the participants favored Explanation (Collection) most, that is, they enumerated supporting reasons after presenting their positions (recall Table 2). More specifically, in L2, 8 participants (72.7%) used Explanation (Collection), whereas in L1, 5 (45.5%) used Explanation (Collection). Furthermore, 4 participants (36.4%) used Explanation (Collection) for both L1 and L2. It is noteworthy that 3 of the 4 participants belonged to the low group. In contrast, the high group showed more variations in their use of L1/L2 organizational patterns. For example, for L1/L2 organizations, one high student used Specification, which has a statement of the main idea as well as a preview statement of supporting reasons before the presentation of the subsequent argument, which requires more detailed planning before writing than Explanation because it should include a preview statement (Hirose, 2003c). No low students used this pattern for either L1 or L2.

The present findings of dominant use of Explanation and slightly more variations in L1 patterns are similar to those of Hirose (2003c) but are somewhat different from Kubota (1998b), who found more variations in the choice of patterns in both L1 and L2. The similar findings with those of Hirose (2003c) are, to be more exact, those of high students' use of organizational patterns (see the High Group's L1 and L2 Organizational Patterns section). The difference between the present study and Kubota (1998b) may be partly accounted for by different writing conditions: Kubota's (1998b) participants wrote at home without any time constraints, whereas the participants in the present study wrote under timed conditions.

(4) Presence or Absence of Summary Statement

As reported above, the results of presence/absence of summary statements in the final section revealed a difference between L1 and L2. More students wrote position statements in L1 than in L2. These results concur with those of Hirose (2003c). On the other hand, the ending with summary statements in L1 does not reflect what some have called a Japanese tendency to avoid perspicuous closure, which leaves it up to the reader to infer the writer's intention (Kobayashi & Rinnert, 1996). The present finding seems to run counter to such a claim. This tendency to end with summary statements may be related to the "bottom-heavy" preference in Japanese (Maynard, 1996). In Japanese, *ryûtô dabi* (literally, "dragon head with snake tail"), which refers to texts that have a bright beginning and end in an anticlimax, is regarded as poor writing (M. Murai, an L1 writing pedagogy specialist, personal communication, March 16, 2001). In light of this view, it is the end that matters in Japanese writing. The present participants' ending with summary statements seems to reflect this end prominent view, and to give support to Japanese preference for "recency and climactic principles" of organization (Okabe, 1983, p. 30).

On the other hand, there was also a tendency to avoid a perspicuous ending in L1. Three high students (Hikari, Ichiro and Jiro) and one low student (Chihiro) finished with a question-form sentence in L1, whereas no students did so in L2. Except one high student (Ichiro), who finished with his proposal in a question form (see Appendix B), the other three (i.e., more than one-fourth of the participants) ended with their position-statements in a question form. Hikari, among others, stated her opinion in the very last sentence for the first time in the form of a rhetorical question called *hango* (see Appendix C). In the present study, some students' L1 compositions were translated by me (Appendixes B, C, D and E). Hirose (2003c) also reported that one of the Japanese participants finished with a position-statement of this question type in Japanese, and implied that finishing with the main idea in the form of a rhetorical question is associated with a good writers' strategy. On the other hand, Jiro and Chihiro did not use the rhetorical question type (see Appendix D for Chihiro's L1 composition). Finishing in the form of a question appears to be in accord with the position of Hinds (1983), who suggests that a Japanese conclusion need not be decisive, but instead indicates doubt or asks a question. On the surface they asked a question, but they probably did not mean to actually raise a question or show doubt because they stated their main idea in the question form. Finishing with such a question form could be regarded as a euphemistic way of stating their opinions as well as of closing their argument. It is interesting that both low and high students resorted to finishing with the main idea in the form of a question in L1. It is also notable that these students who finished with question forms did not transfer this use into L2. Thus, ending with a question form may be characteristic of L1 Japanese writers.

These findings from the analysis of organizational patterns are also discussed in the *Research Question Set 3* section, in which processes involved in organization planning are analyzed. The findings regarding organizational patterns in the two groups are each discussed separately below.

(5) The High Group's L1 and L2 Organizational Patterns

Regarding the location of main ideas, in L1 half of the high group stated their positions in the introduction section, and the other half in the final section. In L2, however, all of them put their position statements in the introduction section. Furthermore, within-subject analysis of macro-level patterns revealed that all except one (Fumi) employed different patterns in L1 and L2. In L2, all high-level students followed deductive type patterns. On the other hand, in L1, they were split into two subgroups, deductive and inductive groups. However, the deductive group all made a summary statement, so that both groups ended with concluding opinion-statements in L1. The two sub-groups' L1 organization scores were not so different: mean score of the inductive group was 70% (21/30), whereas that of the deductive group was 74.4% (22.3/30). Similarly, the mean total score of the inductive group was 69.6% (125.3/180), whereas that of the deductive group was 73.1% (131.7/180). Differences in the rhetorical patterns did not seem to have had much influence on organization score, nor on total score in L1.[15] Summary statement analysis revealed that in L1 all of them made a position or summary statement in the final section, whereas in L2 only half of them did so. All except one (Ginko) also differed regarding the presence of a summary statement.

Overall, as the combined results of the three types of analyses showed, high-level students used different patterns of organization in L1 and L2, and their L1 compositions exhibited more variation. These results seem to accord with those of a previous study (Hirose, 2003c). In terms of L2 proficiency level and L2 writing instructional background, the high group in the present study roughly corresponded to the participants of Hirose (2003c), although the former group's L2 proficiency level was higher than that of the latter as manifested in their total CELT mean score 240.3 as opposed to 205.4.

(6) The Low Group's L1 and L2 Organizational Patterns

Different from the case of the high group, similarities between L1 and L2 organizational patterns were more evident in the case of the low group. In fact, 4 out of 5 low-level students had the same opinion-statement positions in L1 and L2, and all except one (Aya) adopted exactly the same macro-level patterns. Thus, low-level students were more likely to use similar organizations in L1 and L2, and more than half of them used deductive rhetorical patterns for both L1 and L2. It is noteworthy that no low students employed inductive patterns either in L1 or in L2 in the present study. Regarding the presence of a summary statement, they showed a similar tendency as the high students did; that is, more students employed it in L1.

In L2, 40% of the low group had either no opinion statement or a middle placement, whereas 60% put the statements in the initial section as all the high students did. As Table 2 shows, the low group had one case of <u>Obscure</u> in the location of main idea in L2. Although the tendency to put the opinion statement in the initial section and to use deductive patterns is less predominant in the case of the low students, we cannot conclude that low students differed markedly from high students in their organizational choices for L2 writing. Thus, there seems to be no clear relation between the choice of rhetorical patterns and learner L2 proficiency level.

Differences between the two groups were found to be more conspicuous in L1 writing because high-level students employed different, whereas low-level students used similar, patterns between L1 and L2. These differences between the two groups are discussed in the *Research Question Set 3* section, where organization-planning processes are examined.

Research Question Set 2: Relations between Organizational Patterns and Composition Scores

(1) Descriptive Statistics and Reliability

Tables 3 and 4 show descriptive statistics for the total scores and the subscores of L1 and L2 compositions, respectively. For the L2 composition subscores and total score, all interrater values (Pearson

Table 3: Means, *SD*s and Ranges of L2 Composition Scores

(total possible)	Content (60)	Organization (40)	Vocabulary (40)	Lang. Use (50)	Mechanics (10)	Total (200)
M	44.8	26.8	26.6	29.1	7.4	134.7
SD	7.3	7.6	6.2	10.8	1.7	32.3
Range	35-57	14-37	15-35	14-43	4-9	82-177

Table 4: Means, *SD*s and Ranges of L1 Composition Scores

(total possible)	Clarity of Theme (30)	Appeal to Readers (30)	Expression (30)	Organization (30)	Knowledge of Lang. Forms (30)	Social Awareness (30)	Total (180)
M	18.7	17.5	19.5	18.2	22.5	19.3	115.6
SD	2.7	3.4	2.5	4.6	3.1	2.2	15.9
Range	16-25	13-23	15-22	11-25	19-26	16-22	95-140

correlation coefficients) were acceptable: content 0.75; organization 0.83; vocabulary 0.80; language use 0.85; mechanics 0.82; total score 0.97. For the L1 composition subscores and total score, most interrater values (Cronbach's alpha) were acceptable: appeal to the readers 0.79; expression 0.72; organization 0.78; knowledge of language forms 0.73; total score 0.82. However, the reliability estimates for the following items were low: clarity of the theme 0.36, social awareness 0.48.[16] These low estimates are not considered because none of these subscores were used or discussed in the later analysis of the present study.

In the present study, the total score was considered to reflect overall text quality in L1/L2. On the surface, there do not seem to be salient differences between the two languages. The total composition means (%) were 67.4 (L2) versus 64.2 (L1).[17] In terms of percentages, overall the participants scored better in L2. The L2 organization mean (%) was 67, whereas the L1 organization mean (%) was 60.7. Nevertheless, the percentage L1/L2 scores should not be compared within the same writer because different scales were used to evaluate L1/L2 compositions and readers' expectations were likely to be different depending on whether the writing was being done in L1 or L2. Thus, the finding that students scored better in L2 did not necessarily mean that they were better writers in L2.

(2) Correlations among L1 and L2 Composition Scores

A Pearson correlation coefficient matrix (Table 5) revealed that all the subscores of L2 composition had significant positive correlations with the L2 total score. Similarly, all subscores of L1 composition had significant positive correlations with the L1 total score. Furthermore, L2 subscores were significantly correlated with each other, and so were L1 subscores except for several items. All the L2 subscores and L2 total

Table 5: Correlation Matrix for L1 and L2 Composition Scores

	1	2	3	4	5	6	7	8	9	10	11	12	13
1 L2 Total	1.00												
2 L2 Content	.97**	1.00											
3 L2 Org.	.98**	.97**	1.00										
4 L2 Voc.	.96**	.92**	.95**	1.00									
5 L2 Lang. Use	.96**	.88**	.91**	.87**	1.00								
6 L2 Mech.	.87**	.78**	.82**	.86**	.83**	1.00							
7 L1 Total	.74**	.68*	.74**	.78**	.65*	.80**	1.00						
8 L1 Theme	.48	.45	.50	.54	.40	.58	.89**	1.00					
9 L1 Appeal	.73**	.68*	.72*	.79**	.66*	.78**	.96**	.88**	1.00				
10 L1 Express.	.64*	.66*	.71*	.64*	.49	.74**	.77**	.57	.68*	1.00			
11 L1 Org.	.65*	.54	.59	.66*	.67*	.74**	.89**	.83**	.88**	.46	1.00		
12 L1 Lang.	.49	.40	.54	.58	.39	.62*	.82**	.61*	.70*	.76**	.65*	1.00	
13 L1 Social	.82**	.89**	.87**	.84**	.66*	.66*	.77**	.65*	.71*	.67*	.56	.50	1.00

*$p<.05$. **$p<.01$.

score had significant correlations with the L1 total score and such subscores as appeal to the readers and social awareness. Because clarity of the theme and social awareness had relatively low reliability estimates, the results concerning these two items should be treated with some caution.

The L1/L2 total scores had significantly positive correlations with each other. This finding is consistent with those of previous studies dealing with Japanese EFL students' L1/L2 writing relationship (e.g., Kamimura, 1996; Kubota, 1998b; Sasaki & Hirose, 1996). Kamimura (1996) found significant correlations between L1 and L2 narrative compositions. Similarly, Sasaki and Hirose (1996) also found significant positive correlations between total scores of L1/L2 argumentative compositions. Thus, in general good writing in L1 corresponded to good writing in L2 (see Figure 4 for a scattergram of L1 and L2 total scores).

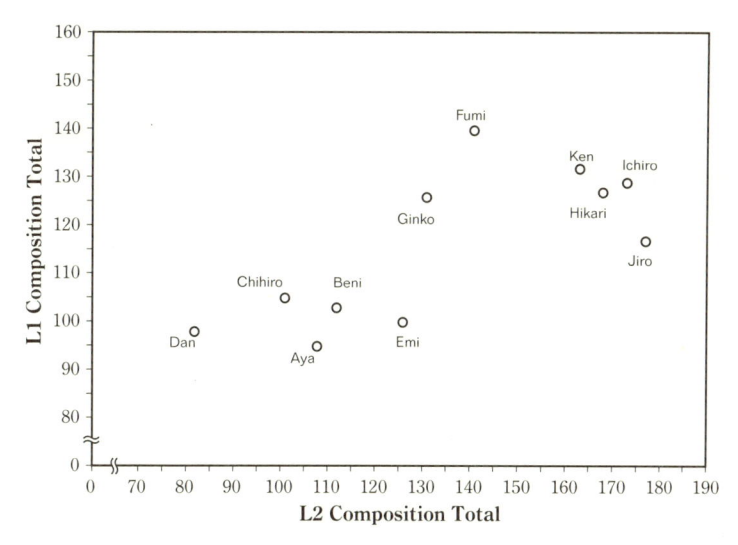

Figure 4: Scattergram of L1 and L2 Total Scores

On the other hand, the finding that there was not a significant correlation between L1 and L2 organization scores is inconsistent with those of previous studies. For example, Kubota (1998b) reported a positive correlation between Japanese and English organization scores on both expository and persuasive topics. The discrepancy found between Kubota (1998b) and the present study can be accounted for in several ways. First, different methods were used to measure students' L1 and L2 writing. In Kubota's comparative study (1998b), organization was evaluated with a range of 5 (excellent) to 1 (poor). Using the same five-point scale for evaluating L1 and L2 compositions might have inflated the correlations between L1 and L2 writing. The lack of significant correlations found between L1 and L2 organizations in the present study might have partly resulted from using different scales that had different points for organization, L1 Japanese (30 points) and L2 English (40 points). The question of which type of scales would be appropriate measures to use for research dealing with more than one language should be further investigated before reaching any consensus. Furthermore, the raters' backgrounds in these studies were also different. Two Japanese professors of education and two English-speaking graduate students of ESL rated the L1 and L2 compositions, respectively, in Kubota (1998b). Three raters specialized in L1 Japanese pedagogy and two English-speaking EFL professors evaluated the L1 and L2 texts, respectively, in the current study. Rater background was found to have significant effects on the evaluation of EFL compositions (Kobayashi & Rinnert, 1996). This could also apply to the assessment of L1 Japanese compositions. Comparative studies of L1/L2 writing would need a much larger number of raters as well as consideration of rater backgrounds. Finally, whether Japanese- and English-speaking readers have different perceptions of what constitutes good organization is another question to be resolved in further studies.

(3) Comparisons of L1 and L2 Organization and Total Scores

Regarding the statistical differences between L1 and L2 organization and total scores, the results of the Wilcoxon Matched-Pairs Signed-Ranks test revealed that the differences were significant in organization ($z=-2.85, p<.025$) but not in total score ($z=-2.22, p>.025$). The L1/L2 total scores were not significantly different from each other. Thus, the relatively better writers in L1 also had relatively higher scores in L2. However, there was a significant difference between L1/L2 organization scores. These findings are interesting in light of the findings of the L1/L2 organizational patterns: that is, the students did not organize L1/L2 compositions similarly.

Figure 5 shows a scattergram of L1/L2 organization scores. Although the two groups' scores were generally separate from each other, one low-level student scored slightly better than one high-level student

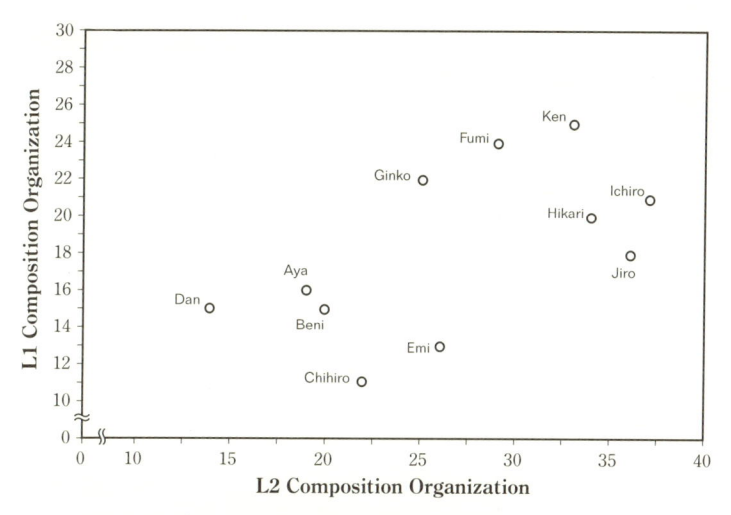

Figure 5: Scattergram of L1 and L2 Organization Scores

(see Figure 5). The figure also revealed that, within each group, good organizers in L2 did not necessarily correspond to those in L1. Among the high-level students, Ichiro, who had the best organization score in L2, ranked fourth in L1 organization score. Similarly, Jiro, the second best L2 organizer, had the lowest organization score in L1. There were also opposite cases of good L1 writers who did not write as well in L2. For example, Fumi, the second best L1 organizer, ranked fifth in the high group in L2. A similar tendency toward diversity seemed to hold true in the case of the low students.

As a final point regarding L1/L2 organization and total scores, it would be interesting to have L2 translations of student L1 compositions as data for comparative analysis. If compatibility between L1 originals and their L2 translations is kept, it would be interesting to have the translated L2 versions evaluated by English writing specialists, and to compare the scores with those of L1 originals evaluated by Japanese specialists. If there are differences between the scores in terms of organization and overall quality, this may mean that Japanese- and English-speaking readers have different perceptions of what constitutes good organizations or good writing.[18]

(4) Comparisons of L1 and L2 Composition Scores between the Two Groups

Tables 6 and 7 show means, *SD*s and ranges of L2 and L1 composition scores, respectively, of the high and low group. As they show, the high group received higher scores in the total score and every subscore of L1/L2 compositions. The results of Mann-Whitney U tests revealed that in L2 the differences between the two groups were significant for total score, vocabulary, language use and mechanics. In L1, on the other hand, the differences between the two groups were significant for total score, clarity of the theme, appeal to the readers, and organization. The high group were significantly better in terms of language-related aspects of L2 writing, whereas they were better in terms of non-linguistic aspects of L1 writing.

In the present study, the total score was considered to reflect overall text quality in L1/L2. The high group obtained significantly higher total scores in both L1 and L2. The L2 total mean (%) was 79.4 (high) versus 52.9 (low), and the L1 total mean (%) was 71.4 (high) versus 55.7 (low). The L2 organization mean (%) was 80.8 (high) versus 50.5 (low), whereas the L1 organization mean (%) was 72.3 (high) versus 46.7 (low). According to Jacobs et al.'s (1981) Profile, the high-level students' total scores (%) corresponded to "Low Advanced," whereas the low students' total scores (%) corresponded to "Low Intermediate" (Hughey, Wormuth,

Table 6: Means, *SD*s and Ranges of L2 Composition Scores according to Group

(total possible)	Content (60)	Organization (40)	Vocabulary (40)	Lang. Use (50)	Mechanics (10)	Total (200)	Range
Low ($n=5$)	38.6 (3.4)	20.2 (4.4)	21.2 (4.1)	20.0 (5.5)	5.8 (1.1)	105.8 (16.1)	82-126
High ($n=6$)	50.0 (5.2)	32.3 (4.5)	31.2 (3.1)	36.7 (7.5)	8.7 (0.5)	158.8 (18.6)	131-177

Note: ( ): *SD*s

Table 7: Means, *SD*s and Ranges of L1 Composition Scores according to Group

(total possible)	Clarity of Theme (30)	Appeal to Readers (30)	Expression (30)	Organization (30)	Knowledge of Lang. Forms (30)	Social Awareness (30)	Total (180)	Range
Low ($n=5$)	16.6 (0.5)	14.4 (1.5)	17.6 (2.7)	14.0 (2.0)	20.2 (1.6)	17.4 (1.7)	100.2 (4.0)	95-105
High ($n=6$)	20.5 (2.4)	20.0 (1.9)	21.2 (0.4)	21.7 (2.6)	24.3 (2.7)	20.8 (1.2)	128.5 (7.6)	117-140

Note: ( ): *SD*s

Hartfiel, & Jacobs, 1983, p. 235). Regarding L1 total scores (%), the high group were considered "good" writers, whereas the low group were between "fair" and "good" writers (Sasaki & Hirose, 1999, p. 477). These results showed that students with higher L2 proficiency level were the better writers in both L1 and L2.

(5) Relations between Organizational Patterns and Evaluation

With regard to the relation between organizational patterns and evaluation, the present study did not lead to the conclusion that the use of deductive patterns resulted in better organization and better text. Although among the whole participant group fewer students chose inductive over deductive patterns in L1, the inductive users all belonged to the high group and earned no lower scores than the deductive users for both the organization and the total scores of their L1 compositions. Thus, the use of inductive patterns did not seem to be directly related to lower evaluation in L1 (cf. Kubota, 1998b). The results also showed the inverse; that is, that the use of deductive patterns either in L1 or L2 did not necessarily lead to higher evaluation of organization and text quality. These results imply that the choice of organizational patterns is not a single factor that contributes to quality of text organization or overall text quality. Other factors such as coherence and connection between/within paragraphs also contribute to the quality of organization, and these other features may carry more weight in evaluation than the choice of organizational patterns does (Kobayashi & Rinnert, 1996).

Research Question Set 3: Comparisons of L1 and L2 Organization-Planning Processes

(1) Organization-Planning Processes

Research Question Set 3 was related to the processes concerning organization planning in L1/L2 writing. In this section, students' protocol data are analyzed within the respective groups to examine how different each group's L1/L2 planning processes are, and to discuss the following findings of the L1/L2 organization analysis: (a) most students, both low and high groups, stated their positions initially and employed a deductive style in L2; (b) some students, especially high-level students, differed in the location of their main ideas between L1 and L2; and (c) students generally showed stronger preference for the presence of a summary statement in L1 than in L2.

(2) The High Group's Processes
1) Similarities between L1 and L2 Processes

The high group's introspective reports revealed that they resorted to comparable organization-planning processes in L1/L2. Before writing, they had decided their positions (for or against) on the given issue, thought of several supporting reasons for their chosen positions, and planned the overall organization along with content (i.e., what to write in the introduction and the middle), without necessarily deciding about the conclusion section. Thus, they all had a global organization plan in mind when they started to write. Before writing in both L1 and L2, 3 of them (60%) made notes, and 2 students engaged in mental planning without writing notes. The remaining student took notes for L2 writing but did not do so for L1 writing. All students who used notes wrote in L1 not only for L1 but also for L2 writing. Because the L2 topic used in the present study (i.e., school uniforms) was related to their experience in Japan, the use of L1 might have been facilitated in the prewriting planning stage.

Thus, their varying organization patterns in L1/L2 did not necessarily result from very different planning processes. For example, before writing in both languages, Hikari had decided on the overall organization and content without making notes. After writing, she reported that she wrote roughly the same as she had planned. In L2, Hikari expressed her opinion explicitly in the beginning sentence and then justified her position with reasons, whereas in L1 she started with Japanese adapting Western culture and customs into her own culture, discussed established Japanese custom celebrating Christmas, and put her opinion in the very last sentence in the form of a rhetorical question, called *hango* (see Appendix C). On the other hand, Ginko planned the organization and wrote the main points down in L1 before writing the first sentence (see Appendix F for Ginko's notes for L1/L2 writing). She wrote L1/L2 texts based on the L1 notes she prepared (see the Total Writing Time and Prewriting Time section in Chapter 3 for more details). Unlike Hikari, her L1/L2 compositions had similar organizational patterns (coded as Explanation, although the subcategories were different). Although they made several changes to their initial plans such as addition and deletion while writing, the high-level students reported their L1/L2 texts were basically written as planned.

2) **Differences between L1 and L2 Processes**

Nevertheless, there were also differences between L1 and L2 writing processes. Writers in the high group tended to make more detailed plans in L2 and to approach L1 writing with more flexibility. Doing more complete planning in L2 was pointed out by half of the high students (Fumi, Jiro, and Ken), and this can be considered as a compensatory strategy to make their L2 writing task easier. With a clear plan at hand (either in mental or written notes), it was likely that they could concentrate on writing their already generated ideas in L2. This strategy probably facilitated the L2 writing, and, with their relatively high L2 proficiency (see Table 1 for their CELT scores), helped them to produce what they wanted to write. They were, in fact, aware that they had little room for integration of new ideas into their initial plan while writing in L2.

To illustrate the present participants' L2 planning, Jiro's case is taken as an example. Jiro reported the following at the end of the initial interview session. He was interrupted at the time when he started writing the first word, and was asked about the sentence, and whether he had a plan for the conclusion and the middle section. Afterwards, he talked about his overall plans of his L2 composition:

> Me: So you have several reasons to justify your position, right?
> Jiro: That's right.
> Me: Aside from the questions I asked you, did you think of anything else after you were given this task?
> Jiro: Aside from what I said?
> Me: Anything except what I asked you just now.
> Jiro: Well, actually I thought of English words.
> Me: What? What do you mean by "English words"?
> Jiro: Given about 30 minutes to write in English, I cannot write much quantitatively. I know I probably cannot include more content than what I told you right now. So I was thinking of English that corresponded to what I thought of.

It appears that Jiro used planning as a self-regulatory strategy. Given the writing task including time allotment, he made calculated decisions about how much content he was able to handle with his limited English ability.

His rigid plans (both content and organization) worked well enough to enable him to write as he planned, probably because his global plans subsequently controlled his L2 writing processes as a monitor. After he finished writing, he did not even reread the whole text unlike those good writers who were reported to reread in previous studies (e.g., Hall, 1990). Thus, the plans seem to have had a more controlling function in L2 writing.

In contrast, the students seem to have generated ideas in L1 with a much less detailed outline, so that they kept the L1 writing process more spontaneous. Fumi, for example, wrote L1 without such a detailed plan as she made for L2, because she felt that "I am confident in writing Japanese, so I think I can manage (without such a plan)." After writing in L1, she commented, "Compared with writing in English, I feel like I did not have a plot to follow. At first I had some plans in my mind. From there, however, many ideas came to mind one after another while I was writing. So I wrote one, then the other and connected these floating ideas this way or that way." She compared L1 and L2 writing processes as follows:

> Fumi: Because I am able to write just as I want to write, Japanese is easier to write in. On the other hand, because I decide what to write before writing, I find the writing stage easier in English.
> Me: Do you usually plan what to write when you write in English?
> Fumi: I've got this feeling that I can't write English unless I plan first. So I make a plan before writing in English.

Those students who planned less in L1 seem to have known that they did not have linguistic (lexical or syntactical) problems while writing. They had an overall sense of direction in L1 composition even when they made a less detailed plan. They could afford to leave L1 writing processes more spontaneous and possibly open for generating new ideas. Once they started implementing their plans into action while writing, even with their linguistic advantages, they had emergent problems of text production. As several high-level students testified, this flexible aspect of L1 writing can cause them difficulties, such as integrating new ideas coherently in the text under construction and maintaining unity, especially within a set time allotment. This less constrained writing process might partly explain why their mean L1 total score (71.4%) was lower than that for L2 total score (79.4%).

Jiro's more spontaneous L1 writing process is worth discussing in this context. Before writing in L1, he had several lines of argument in mind, deliberately leaving details undecided before writing in L1, and reported that he had decided to write thinking about them while writing. After he finished, he said he was able to start that way because he was confident of verbalizing his thoughts in L1. On the other hand, he also reported that he failed in organizing his arguments, especially the introductory paragraph as follows:

> Jiro: Probably because I am aware of limitations in my English writing ability, I have a set technique in writing English. I know in English I have to make a concluding remark in the beginning.
> Me: Uh-huh.
> Jiro: So I usually put this into practice. Then a kind of conclusion statement is summarized in a paragraph form in the end. It's quite easy.
> Me: How about in Japanese?
> Jiro: In Japanese, the beginning is like entering in a roundabout way.
> Me: What do you mean by "entering in a roundabout way"? When I interrupted your writing and asked you what you were going to

write, you answered you were going to start with a general statement.

Jiro: Yes. Probably that was the wrong start. I should have written straightforwardly just like in English.

Me: You feel you should have written that way in Japanese too?

Jiro: That's right.

Me: Does the opening influence the flow to the conclusion?

Jiro: I felt so . . . .

After writing in L1, Jiro reported he found it difficult to make paragraphs, especially a concluding paragraph, and could not accomplish it. He owed his failure to make a concluding paragraph to the roundabout way he started in L1. His perceived failure is evidenced by his lower L1 total score (65%), as opposed to his L2 score (88.5%), and his lower L1 organization score (60%) as opposed to L2 organization score (90%). His L2 total score was the best, whereas his L1 total score was the worst in the high group. Similarly, his L2 organization was the second best, whereas his L1 organization score was the lowest in the group. His low L1 scores might have derived from lack of planning for L1 writing and his choice of an inductive style, as he himself implied.

Nevertheless, flexible aspects of L1 writing did not necessarily lead writers to produce lower quality texts. In contrast with Jiro, Fumi, who also made a less detailed outline in L1, had the best L1 composition score in the group. In both L1 and L2, she placed her opinion statements initially and used deductive patterns (recall Table 2).

High students' more detailed planning in L2 runs counter to the findings of previous research. In a review of past empirical L1/L2 writing studies, Silva (1993) concluded that "overall, L2 writers did less planning, at the global and local level" (p. 661). Examining ESL students' perceptions of differences in L1/L2 writing, Silva (1992) also found that planning was one of the salient areas of such differences. The students in his study reportedly perceived greater difficulty in planning in L2. Thus, the implications of the present study about plans functioning as a stronger control over writing process seem to provide an interesting aspect of planning strategy specific to L2 writing and thus require further discussion (see Part II).

3) Discussion in Light of the Findings of Organizational Analysis

The findings regarding organizational analysis that should be discussed related to L1/L2 organization-planning processes are: (a) all high-level students organized their L2 compositions in deductive ways; (b) half of them organized L1 compositions inductively; and (c) half did not write a summary statement in L2 (recall Table 2 for more details of their organizational patterns). Analysis of both the L2 organizational patterns they used and processes involved in organizing L2 compositions showed that they knew deductive patterns were preferred in English. It can be speculated that L2 instruction and L2 writing experience helped them to learn to use the preferred patterns.

Jiro explained about organizing his L2 composition as follows:

I know in English we should make a conclusive-type statement in the beginning, and I actually put this into practice. Then it turned out I had a concluding paragraph almost automatically in the end.

Similarly, Ichiro, who had studied English at a college in the United States in addition to having studied at a Japanese university, reported that he had written his first paragraph in L2 with ease. He did not start his introductory paragraph with his position statement, but with his acknowledgment of the opposing views of the American readers (see

Appendix B). It was in the last sentence of the first paragraph that he stated his position regarding the issue. According to Rinnert and Kobayashi (2001), the introductory paragraph of English essays "tend[s] to contain a thesis statement toward or at the end of the introduction" (p. 201). In his protocols, he explained that he had learned to place the thesis statement in this position in an English composition class in the United States.

The students seemed to have procedurized knowledge of organizational structure in English (i.e., statement of a position, its justification with reasons, and summary/restatement in the conclusion). Once they made plans for their positions and reasons, organizing them in L2 was not a problem for the students. In addition to stating their positions in the first paragraph, they were also fully aware of making a summary statement in the final paragraph. Regarding summary statements, half of the high group did not make the statement (recall Table 2); however, this does not mean they did not consider making one. Right after writing in L2, Ichiro expressed his concerns about not having included a concluding paragraph. In fact, he tried to write one, but he decided not to do so because he was supposed to be writing a letter to the editor, not an essay. He was still a little worried whether his decision was right, because he knew it was conventional to make a concluding statement in English essays. Apart from such an intentional decision, there was also a possibility of a mismatch between the writer's intended meaning and the expressed meaning. Fumi intended to finish with a summary statement, but expressed her dissatisfaction with her supposedly concluding sentence as follows: "I took great pains to discuss this issue, but I have found my last sentence too simple, lacking in detail, and insufficient." The sentence, "These are my reasons that I take this side," was not coded as a summary statement because it did not re-present her position or summarize what was discussed. Evidenced by the gap she felt, this sentence did not express her intended meaning sufficiently. This type of gap was probably due to the writer's L2 proficiency level or to her writing ability being insufficient to express the intended meaning.

    Contrastively, in L1, the students appeared not to use a similar type of organizational pattern. Ken, who started with an opinion-statement in L2, explained that the notion of topic sentence had not occurred to him when writing in L1. Asked why it came to his mind while writing only in L2, he attributed it to two factors: (a) such deductive patterns were taught as typical of English texts in L2 writing instruction; (b) he had been familiarized with such patterns through L2 reading experience. Although they decided their positions and reasons to justify them, it is noteworthy that some high-level students experienced more difficulty in organizing L1 compositions. In particular, writing the first paragraph was not easy (recall Jiro's sense of failure felt for his L1 composition, especially for the first paragraph). Ichiro, who wrote the first paragraph in L2 with no difficulty, encountered the problem of writing the first paragraph in L1 as follows:

> Me: This is the very beginning, right?
> Ichiro: Yes, I was wondering how to start.
> Me: You told me you were planning to state your position first. Were you concerned about how to express it?
> Ichiro: Yeah, I wondered how to start the first sentence. In short, I am against this issue after all. But strictly speaking, I don't belong to either side. I have a neutral opinion on this issue. So the conclusion was going in a different direction.
> Me: Pardon me?
> Ichiro: At first I wanted to write, "I'm against it" from the beginning, but (Me: Yes) I actually wrote somewhat gently

something like "Although I have a neutral opinion, I would rather take a negative position."

Me: You began that way?

Ichiro: Yes, at the beginning.

Me: It's quite complicated, isn't it? Your position is against the issue, though.

Ichiro: Yes.

Me: You didn't simply write, "I am against it."

Ichiro: No, not bluntly. (Me: No.) I have been immersed in such a culture that I can't deny an issue so abruptly.

Me: Do you really mean you are against the issue?

Ichiro: To me the present Japanese customs of Christmas are strange, so . . . .

Me: You think that way, but . . . (Ichiro: Right.) you stated your position gently . . . .

Ichiro: That's right. But I expressed my position.

Me: You didn't write, "I'm against it," did you?

Ichiro: I wrote my stance clearly in the conclusion.

In L1, Ichiro seems to have disclosed his hesitancy in expressing his position explicitly in the first paragraph (see Appendix B). Although the main idea was coded as placed at the initial position in L1 (recall Table 2), he in fact made his explicit statement ("I am against the present Japanese custom concerning Christmas.") in the conclusion section.

Japanese students' hesitation to make a definite statement or difficulty in writing introductions acceptable to English-speaking readers has been reported in previous research (e.g., Hirose, 1992; Oi, 1986; Silva, 1992). The present study revealed some advanced Japanese EFL students had such problems in L1, but not in L2. Similarly, Hirose (2003c) found that some Japanese writers started with neutral or personal information related to the topic in L1, suggesting that they probably needed this type of springboard statement to avoid arguing the issue from the very beginning. It is interesting that Ichiro, who studied English in the United States as well as in Japan, was reluctant to make an explicit statement in the beginning in L1. The findings of the present study suggest that it is not so difficult for EFL Japanese students to learn to use deductive patterns or to make a general statement in the beginning in L2, whereas it is not so easy for some to do the same in L1.

The present study also found that finishing with the summary statement was more favorably perceived in L1 writing. Finishing with the main idea in an inductive pattern was likely to require more elaborate skills on the part of writers, as Jiro's L1 writing compared to his L2 writing manifested. Although the use of an inductive pattern in L1 was associated with the good writer group in the present study, it did not lead to better organization scores automatically. Similarly, finishing with the main idea in the form of a rhetorical question can be associated with a good writers' strategy (recall Appendix C for Hikari's L1 composition). This type of ending may be a strategic choice. In Japanese, the use of rhetorical questions is considered an effective way of claiming one's opinion politely and also a rhetorical way of closing an argument (see Hirose, 2003c).

These confounding results between L1 and L2 can be interpreted in several ways. First, the students apparently used their learned knowledge of stating the main ideas initially in L2. They might have overgeneralized the rule about the topic sentence in the initial position in English. In contrast, in L1 they did not seem to be conscious of that rule to the same degree as in L2, which induced more variations in their organizational patterns in L1. In a comparative study of structures of letters of request, Hirose (1990) found that Japanese EFL students adopted more varied rhetorical types when writing in L1 compared with when writing in L2. Thus, when writing in L1, the students utilized the language more freely than when writing in L2. Second, related to the first point, students used less conscious, more spontaneous writing processes in L1. Lack of consciousness over the placement of the main point in the initial position was likely to induce the use of inductive style. It was also likely that their tendency to avoid making an explicit statement in the beginning reinforced positioning the main point in the final section. Third, different groups of readers were presupposed when they wrote in L1 and L2. This was exactly why Ichiro could not make an explicit position statement in L1. In fact, Ichiro pointed out that he always had the American reader in mind while writing in English. For him, writing in English meant writing to non-Japanese readers. He had written essays for an American teacher who taught English composition classes. L2 writing experience had fostered awareness of an English-speaking audience. While writing in L2, he was conscious of readers with a different cultural background from Japanese. Thus, awareness of audience might have also affected high-level students' choice of organizational patterns.

(3) The Low Group's Processes

The low group's organization-planning processes were different from those of the high group in both languages. Different from the high students, they expressed discrepancies between what they wanted to write at first and what they produced in the end. They felt different types of mismatch between L1 and L2. In L1, 3 of them said that while writing they went in a "different" direction and the content became too big for the given topic. In L2, all of them confessed they could not write to a sufficiently satisfactory level. Chihiro, for example, reported that he managed writing down only half of what he wanted to write. Perceiving such gaps in L2 implies they had some initial plans, which were not implemented to their fulfillment, probably due to their limited L2 proficiency level that was insufficient to express their intended meaning especially under a time limit. The problem of gaps was shared by high-level students, but not as massively as low-level students (recall Fumi's dissatisfaction with her concluding sentence).

As in the case of L1/L2 organizational patterns, similarities were more evident between L1/L2 organization-planning processes. Their introspective accounts revealed that some low students wrote L1/L2 texts without global organization plans. For example, Emi, who put her position in the middle section in L1/L2 (recall Table 2), seemed to start writing when she hit upon something to write about. For L2, she first wrote an L1 text, slightly more detailed than the final L2 text, sentence by sentence. After writing an L1 sentence, she then translated it into an L2 sentence. In L1, she prepared no such notes to cling to. It is notable that Emi scored best in the low group in terms of L2 organization and total score.

As Emi's sentence-by-sentence preparation for L2 writing showed, low-level students were likely to be tied up with what to write next, and to devote themselves to local planning (e.g., at a phrase, clause or sentence level). Aya, for example, first wrote two L1 sentences in notes, translated them into L2 one by one, but perceived a mismatch between her intended meaning and the expressions she managed to retrieve from her L2 knowledge. For example, her prepared notes included an L1 word for "discrimination," but she could not translate it into L2. Then she decided to write what came to mind directly in L2 because she "felt it even more difficult to translate the prepared Japanese sentence into English." Local planning in L2 seemed to derive from L1 writing strategies because these students thought and wrote without global planning in L1 too. This type of spontaneous writing process may lead to producing texts that reflect a writer's stream of consciousness and have a danger of becoming divergent in scope (recall that some low-level students perceived the text went out of control while writing).

Nevertheless, there were some low-level students who formulated conscious organization plans for L1/L2. Before writing in L2, Beni decided on her position and took notes on it with reasons in L1 (see Appendix G for Beni's notes for L1/L2 writing). She made a similar plan while writing in L1 and explained about the pattern as follows: "When we write an opinion-stating essay, it's necessary to state our position first and then justify it with appropriate reasons. I probably learned this in high school." Her reflective reports implied that she learned to locate the main point at the initial position in L1 writing instruction. There is a strong likelihood that she transferred her learned L1 rhetorical strategy into L2 writing. Her L1/L2 texts were judged to have the same intended rhetorical structure [coded as <u>Explanation (Collection)</u>]. Thus, Beni's case suggests that the effects of writing instruction have been transferred across languages. However, although she managed to organize her L1/L2 texts as she had planned, her organization scores were not the best in the low group: 50% (15/30) in L1 and 50% (20/40) in L2. This finding suggests that mere possession of "an opinion-essay schema that contains only two elements—*statement of belief* and *reason*" (Bereiter & Scardamalia, 1987, p. 8) and its implementation—position-stating in the introduction and supporting the position with reasons—does not necessarily lead to better organized essays.

Similarly but more strategically, Dan attempted to write both L1 and L2 texts with a *ki-shô-ten-ketsu* pattern in mind, and explained about the pattern as follows: stating the writer's position (*ki*), giving supporting reasons for his position (*shô*), introducing a counterargument and opposing it with further reasons (*ten*), and restating his position (*ketsu*). According to this basic pattern, the topic is introduced in *ki*, developed in *shô*, then a transition is made in *ten*, and the topic is concluded in *ketsu*. His adaptations of this pattern to argumentative texts are exactly in accordance with those exemplified in *Kokugo Hyôgen*, Japanese writing textbooks at high school (e.g., Ôoka et al., 1998). This adapted pattern of *ki-shô-ten-ketsu* is not particularly confined to Japanese but can be generally applied to other languages such as English. If successfully applied, it might have led to the Explanation (Comparison) or Specification (Comparison) (see Appendix A). Despite his intention, however, Dan's L1/L2 texts were not considered to have this particular pattern [coded as Explanation (Collection)]. This mismatch could partly explain his low organization scores, 50% (15/30) in L1 and 35% (14/40) in L2. His L1 organization score was the second best, whereas his L2 score was the lowest in the low group. Similarly, Chihiro also reported having applied a *ki-shô-ten-ketsu* pattern to his L1/L2 texts, which did not show the intended pattern either (see Appendix D). His L1 organization score was the lowest [36.7% (11/30)], whereas his L2 organization score was the second best [55% (22/40)] in the low group. In L1, his opinion statement was positioned finally, but the organizational pattern was not coded Induction but Other. In L2, his opinion statement was not clearly stated (therefore, coded as Obscure), and the organizational pattern did not fit any of the categories used (thus, coded as Other). He appears to have evidenced problems in organizing both L1 and L2 compositions.

    In sum, the results of process analysis showed that low-level students used similar organization planning strategies in L1 and L2, suggesting that they tended to transfer L1 organization strategies to L2. Some appeared to use similar organizational patterns such as statement of one's position followed by its justification and *ki-shô-ten-ketsu*, whereas others wrote without such patterns. Thus, the results showed that some low-level students did pay some attention to organization while writing in L1 and L2. However, their organization scores for their compositions in both languages did not differ much from those of students who were not conscious of organization. Concerns over organization while writing did not lead them to write texts with better organization. This finding should be taken into consideration in relation to another finding that their organizational patterns did not necessarily reflect their intended patterns.

Summary of Part I

By examining not only organizational patterns of compositions but also writing processes of each individual student, the present chapter disclosed the following findings:

1. Independent of L2 proficiency level or past L2 writing experience, most students in this study employed deductive type rhetorical patterns in L2, which were apparently derived from either transfer from learned L1 strategies or use of learned L2 strategies. Therefore, past writing instruction in either L1 or L2 seems to have affected their choice of L2 organizational patterns. This finding implies that the effects of L1/L2 writing instruction on student writing can be bidirectional.
2. The high-level students all organized L2 compositions in deductive ways. Whereas they were aware of linguistic limitations in L2, they had procedurized knowledge of organizational patterns of English argumentative writing, and some actually found organizing L2 compositions easier than those of L1.
3. In L1, the students also used the deductive style, although to a lesser degree, which did not support the claim that Japanese writers prefer inductive style (see Kubota, 1992, for an extensive review). The inductive style was employed only by high-level students only in L1. The students with higher writing ability in both languages tended to choose different organizational patterns, whereas the low-level students used similar patterns in L1 and L2. The L1 compositions were organized in more varied ways probably due to the more spontaneous nature of writing processes. As students become more experienced in L2 writing or acquired more control of L2 writing skills, they may afford to employ more diverse organizational patterns in L2 too (see Chapter 5 for student L2 text with inductive organization). Another explanation of their not writing the same way in L1 as in L2 (i.e., not stating their position explicitly in the introduction)

may be that they had different readers in mind, Japanese in L1 and English speakers in L2. It is dangerous to be too conclusive about these findings. As the findings imply, however, the same writer can choose different organizational patterns regardless of language, and preferred patterns may differ depending on the writer/reader, not on L1 or L1 cultures.

4. In regard to L2 organization, this study found no clear relation between student L2 proficiency level and organizational patterns either. The result suggests that students with limited L2 proficiency can produce a deductive style by transferring L1 patterns such as *ki-shô-ten-ketsu* into L2. As discussed, this pattern can be adaptable to argumentative writing and is not specific to Japanese (cf. Hinds, 1983). If rhetorical patterns of argumentative texts do not differ according to language, L2 students should be taught to transfer L1 strategies into L2 writing. The issue of transferability of L1 rhetorical patterns into L2 and vice versa also needs to be pursued in follow-up studies.

5. There was no relation found between organizational patterns and evaluation of writing quality. In L2, the great majority of participants, regardless of L2 proficiency levels, resorted to deductive organization and its reliance did not necessarily lead to good evaluation. In L1, half of the high students chose inductive organization, and the high group gained significantly better organization scores than the low group.

6. Concerning students' choices of organizational patterns, the results of the present analysis implied that such multi-faceted factors as students' perceptions about good organization, students' developmental level in writing, task variables including the time conditions and topics, and the perceived relationship between the reader and the writer exerted inevitable influences on their L1/L2 writing.

7. Although differences in organization-planning processes of the two student groups were focused on in the present chapter, their L2 writing processes also included similar writing strategies, such as writing notes in L1 before writing. Even high-level students made use of L1 in the planning stage. Preparing notes in L1 can be a good strategy not only to facilitate

idea-generation but also to organize the generated ideas especially in a limited time. Although the extent or function of L1 use can be different depending on the group, the use of L1 in the planning stage may be a necessary part of the L2 writing process for both groups.
8. High proficiency level Japanese EFL students were found to be good writers not only of L2 but also of L1. This finding shows that L2 proficiency is related to L1 writing ability as well as L2 writing ability. It is consistent with the findings of previous studies dealing with Japanese EFL students (e.g., Sasaki & Hirose, 1996), but is inconsistent with those dealing with ESL students (e.g., Raimes, 1987). This discrepancy can be partly explained by different L1 instructional background among participants of those studies. Compared with the ESL students studying in the U.S., including those who had no L1 instruction, the Japanese EFL students had relatively similar L1 instructional background.
9. Needless to say, however, we have to be cautious about drawing any conclusions based on a small sample size, and these results should be confirmed with a larger sample of participants.

Part II

Investigating
L1 and L2 Writing Processes

Chapter 2
L1 and L2 Writing Processes of Low L2 Proficiency Level Students

Previous Studies of L1 and L2 Writing Processes

Compared with writing product research, much fewer studies have investigated how people write. It is only since the early 1980's that cognitive psychologists have taken up writing process for research. According to Uchida (1989), the first study that examined writing process was Hayes and Flower (1980). Using protocol analysis, they built a model of writing process, and then Flower and Hayes (1981) presented a similar writing model. This is considered a writing model of competent L1 writers. Its writing process consists of three basic processes of planning, translating, and reviewing, which are all under control of monitoring. Translating, in their sense, refers to "the process of putting ideas into visible language" (Flower & Hayes, 1981, p. 373), not to that of expressing the sense of words in another language. As the writers write, they do not proceed through these three processes in a fixed linear order. In other words, the writing process is considered a recursive process. Furthermore, these processes also have sub-processes. For example, idea generating, organizing and goal-setting are sub-processes of planning. These sub-processes are embedded within other processes, and thus the writing process is hierarchically organized in the model. As Flower and Hayes (1981) considered it "a working hypothesis and springboard for further research" (p. 366), their model has been probably the most frequently discussed and quoted model in writing research. Hayes (1996) presented a revised writing model incorporating empirical findings made since the first model (1980).

Subsequently, Bereiter and Scardamalia (1987) proposed two models of writing, namely the "knowledge-telling" and "knowledge-transforming" models. Contrasts between the two models were drawn using the following pairs of descriptors: "everyday thinking" versus "formal reasoning," "casual reading" versus "critical reading," and "talking" versus "oratory" (Bereiter & Scardamalia, 1987, p. 6). The former descriptors of these pairs are all associated with "novice" writers' processes and the latter of the pairs with "expert" writers' processes. According to the "knowledge-telling" model, the writers, just like in ordinary conversation, tell their knowledge without much planning or goal-setting. A 12-year-old writer described such a writing process as follows:

> I have a whole bunch of ideas and write down until my supply of ideas is exhausted. Then I might try to think of more ideas up to the point when you can't get any more ideas that are worth putting down on paper and then I would end it. (Bereiter & Scardamalia, 1987, p. 9)

This approach to writing is contrasted with the more complex "knowledge-transforming" model, in which the writers transform their knowledge by rethinking and restating their ideas until they fully develop their thoughts and create a text. Thus, the "knowledge-transforming" model involves the writer's continuously developing both knowledge and text. These two writing models have been validated with empirical evidence, although much remains to be explored. For example, how the writer's knowledge is transformed and integrated into new forms of knowledge in text creating process has not yet been elucidated (Sugimoto, 1989).

In Japan, too, cognitive psychologists have attempted to uncover writing processes since the early 1980's. Anzai and Uchida (1981), which examined Japanese elementary pupils' L1 writing processes using reflective protocol analysis, is a notable example of such process research. Nevertheless, research to date has not yet fully addressed highly cognitive processes of writing (Sugimoto, 1989).

Following L1 writing process research, research has started to capture L2 writing process employing similar methodologies used in L1 research. In Japan, however, writing process research has been scarcely done in the L2 writing field, and process research is extremely limited (Momoi, 2001). Although L2 models of writing process have not been proposed yet, L2 writing process research has been prolifically conducted mostly in the United States, and the participants were mainly ESL students studying there (e.g., Raimes, 1985; Zamel, 1983). Such L2 process studies have yielded findings similar to those of L1 process studies (see Krapels, 1990, for an extensive review). That is, L2 good writers were found to resort to similar writing processes as L1 counterparts. Similarly, L2 weak writers' writing processes corresponded to those of L1 weak writers. These findings were drawn from studies that examined L1 and L2 writers, respectively.

Process research should further investigate L1/L2 writing as a within-subject phenomenon. Such research makes an important step in investigating how an individual student writes in L1/L2 and whether each student's L1/L2 writing processes are similar. Some studies have actually compared L1 and L2 writing processes within the same writers. Such previous research has found both similarities and differences between L1 and L2 writing processes. Many studies have found similarities between L1 and L2 writing, for example, in planning (Jones & Tetroe, 1987), attention paid to various aspects of writing (Cumming, 1989) and revising (Hall, 1990). Use of common strategies in L1/L2 suggests that L1 writing strategies are transferred to L2 writing. In spite of these findings that provided evidence for such transfer, the transfer of writing strategies from L1 to L2 is still an inconclusive issue. In her review article of L2 writing process research, Krapels (1990) called for research to investigate "transfer of composing ability across language" (p. 53).

Although still small in number, L1/L2 writing processes of EFL students have been also investigated using a within-subject design. Arndt (1987), who examined 6 advanced Chinese EFL students' L1/L2 writing processes using a within-subject design, found similarities between the two processes within individual writers. If a writer's L2 proficiency is limited, however, it may hinder L2 writing process in such a way that the writer is unable to write the way the writer does in L1. Although participant L2 proficiency level was not reported, Uzawa (1996) compared inexpert Japanese students' L1 writing, L2 writing and translation from L1 into L2 processes using a think-aloud method. She revealed that the focus of attention of participants during L1/L2 writing was "unexpectedly very similar" (p. 283). In both L1 and L2, for example, their attention to language use was very low, whereas their metacognitive attention was high. These two previous studies reported mostly similarities between the two processes.

Differences between L1 and L2 writing processes were also reported in past research. In a review article of empirical studies of L1/L2 writing, Silva (1993) concluded that despite similarities found, there were also salient differences between L1 and L2 writing in terms of both written product features and writing processes. For example, the previous research indicated that L2 products were shorter (fewer words) and contained more errors, and that pauses were more frequent, longer, and more time-consuming during L2 writing. Based on these findings, Silva (1993) argued that L2 writing is "more constrained, more difficult, and less effective" (p. 668) and called for further research to capture the unique nature of L2 writing. With the recognition of similarity between L1 and L2 writing, Leki (1992) also suggested we should shed more light on differences between L1 and L2 writers. These differences, however, have not been fully investigated in L2 writing process research.

The mixed results of previous studies concerning the L1/L2 writing processes might arise partly from the multi-faceted aspects of L2 writing. As discussed in Part I, L2 texts represent various factors including not only writers' L2 writing ability, proficiency level, writing experience, and instructional background, but also L1 counterparts of these factors. Moreover, past studies also showed that writing processes reflect individual differences even among a small number of participants (e.g., Arndt, 1987; Raimes, 1985). Among the variables affecting L2 writing, the participants' L2 proficiency and L1 writing ability levels have been found to exert an influence on Japanese EFL students' L2 writing ability (Hirose & Sasaki, 1994). Thus, when L1 and L2 writing processes are compared within an individual participant, L2 proficiency and L1 writing levels of participants should be controlled. It appears necessary to control L2 proficiency and/or L1 writing level when transferability of writing strategies is examined between L1 and L2 writing. Despite similarities reported in previous research, it still remains to be explored whether L1/L2 writing processes are similar regardless of their L2 proficiency or L1 writing level. Thus, Part II of the present volume investigates Japanese EFL students' L1/L2 writing processes by controlling student L2 proficiency/L1 writing level.

The present chapter compares L1/L2 writing processes of low-level students. Because lower proficiency Japanese EFL students were found to be weaker writers not only in L2 but also in L1 (Sasaki & Hirose, 1996), limited L2 proficiency may not be the sole hindering factor for L2 writing, which can also be influenced by inefficient L1 writing skills. Thus, it was considered necessary to compare L1 and L2 writing processes of low-proficiency students using a within-subject design. In order to explore strategies and knowledge students used while writing, the present study examined stimulated recall protocols of what they did during pauses. Using a similar methodology, Bosher (1998) explored pausing behavior of ESL students, and suggested the methodology was valid and reliable. Like previous studies that investigated protocols of 3 participants (Bosher, 1998) or 6 participants (Arndt, 1987), this study took a case-study approach. Unlike these studies, however, process analysis was complemented by product analysis in this study.

Research Questions

The present chapter compares the low students' L2 English writing with L1 Japanese writing in terms of writing processes, and examines to what extent their L2 writing processes are similar to that of L1 writing.[1] It addresses the following research questions:

Are there differences in low proficiency level Japanese EFL students' processes of L1 and L2 writing? If so, how and to what extent do their L2 writing processes differ from L1 writing processes?

Method

Participants

As in Chapter 1, 5 first-year Japanese university students comprised the low group in the present study. The participants were solicited from among 62 students enrolled in English classes taught by me in 1997, based on their CELT scores (Table 1). Making reference to the CELT scores of the weak writer group (mean total score = 145.9) in a previous study (Sasaki & Hirose, 1996), those students with a CELT total score of 150 or below were asked if they could participate in the research outside class and they were financially compensated for their time. The participants' L2 proficiency level was low-intermediate (recall Table 1; CELT $M=127.8$, $SD=11.8$, range=110 to 142). They had studied English for 6 years through the Japanese school system. They also shared a similar L2 writing background in that they had had little English writing experience before.[2] The participants did not differ very much in terms of age, academic major, previous educational background in L1/L2, and L2 proficiency level.

Data

(1) Writing Products

In addition to the end-products of L1/L2 compositions, the participants' preliminary notes and outlines were also collected (see Appendixes F and G for students' sample notes and compositions).

(2) Writing Processes

As explained in the Data section in Chapter 1, the stimulated recall protocols were collected following a procedure adapted from that of Anzai and Uchida (1981). Concurrent think-aloud protocols (i.e., describing aloud what the writers are doing while engaging with the writing process) were not collected mainly because the concurrent method was believed to interfere with normal writing processes tremendously, especially when writing in L2. I was also aware of the criticisms reflective recall protocols are exposed to. That is, recall protocols reflect only what the writers do while pausing, excluding what they do when they are not pausing. Furthermore, some argue that, because they report what they think they were doing, students' retrospective reports may not be consistent with what they actually did during pausing, and that there is no way to confirm the consistency between what they did and what they think they did, due to the time lag. It is also possible for them to forget what they were doing while pausing. Regarding the consistency problem, Uchida (1990) pointed out that a participant's explanation of what s/he was doing during pausing evidenced the participant's knowledge of what s/he was supposed to be doing at the time of pausing, and the participant's possession of such knowledge suggests that s/he is able to use that knowledge when s/he encounters a similar problem to solve in another situation (see Greene & Higgins, 1994, for the advantages of the retrospective method).

Instead of forcing them to think aloud while writing, the writing sessions were videotaped starting from when the students were handed a task sheet up until they said they had finished writing. They were interrupted at the time when they started writing the first word, and they were asked about the first sentence and whether they had a plan for the conclusion and the middle section. Immediately after they finished writing, students were asked follow-up questions to examine whether their responses to the prewriting interview questions matched their actual writing or not. Thus, the same questions were asked twice to confirm if their responses were consistent and thus provide reliable data for analysis. Then they viewed the videotapes together with me. Their pauses of several seconds during writing were focused on in the follow-up interviews. I asked questions about their thoughts during these pauses in the videotaped writing process. All these question/answer sessions, conducted in L1, were audiotaped and later transcribed for process analysis. The data collection took approximately 2 hours per participant.

Data Analysis

(1) Writing Products

As explained in Chapter 1, L1 and L2 compositions were scored according to their respective writing scales (see the Data section in Chapter 1). In addition, the overall length of L1/L2 compositions was measured by counting the total number of words/characters, sentences and paragraphs per composition. Because English and Japanese have different graphical systems, it is not possible to compare composition lengths by the same measure other than sentence and paragraph.[3] Following the standard procedures in each language, every word was counted for English, whereas every character, *kanji* (Chinese character), *hiragana* and *katakana*, was counted for Japanese. Although analysis of L1/L2 writing processes is the focus of Part II, product analysis is also used to complement process analysis.

(2) Writing Processes

The videotapes and transcribed data were used for the pause analysis, and participants' responses were coded based on the scheme used in Anzai and Uchida (1981) (see Appendix H for a full description of each category; all categories were translated by me). This coding scheme was also used in a study that investigated EFL Japanese students' L2 writing processes (Sasaki, 2000) and was considered a useful means to investigate L1/L2 writing processes of Japanese students.

An EFL lecturer who was independent of this research and I coded 7 participants' L1 and L2 protocols (63.6%) randomly selected from the total protocols. There was 90.4% agreement between the two coders. Discrepancies found between the two coders were resolved through discussion. The remaining 4 participants' protocols (36.4%) were coded by me. In addition, the total time spent and prewriting time (time spent before writing the first sentence) were measured (Raimes, 1985).

Results and Discussion

L1 and L2 Writing Products

Tables 8 and 9 show each participant's L2 and L1 composition scores, respectively. The total score mean was 105.8 (52.9%) in L2 and 100.2 (55.7%) in L1. In terms of percentages, their L1 writing scores were slightly better than their L2 scores, but there were no noticeable differences between them. Three students obtained better scores in L1, whereas 2 students obtained better scores in L2. Different scales were used to measure students' L1 and L2 writing; thus, results of such comparisons should be treated with caution. Nevertheless, it is noteworthy that their L1 and L2 writing levels did not seem to differ much. According to the interpretative guide that accompanied the ESL Composition Profile, their L2 mean (52.9) was regarded as "Low

Intermediate" (Hughey et al., 1983, p. 235). Similarly, with regard to the L1 writing mean (55.6), they belonged somewhere between "fair" and "good" writers (Sasaki & Hirose, 1999, p. 477). Generally, there was less variation in L1 total scores (95 to 105) than in their L2 counterparts (82 to 126). Furthermore, the *SD*s of L2 subscores were larger than those of L1.

Table 8: L2 Composition Scores of the Low Group

(total possible)	Content (60)	Organization (40)	Vocabulary (40)	Lang. Use (50)	Mechanics (10)	Total (200)
Aya	37	19	22	24	6	108
Beni	38	20	23	24	7	112
Chihiro	39	22	20	14	6	101
Dan	35	14	15	14	4	82
Emi	44	26	26	24	6	126
Mean	38.6	20.2	21.2	20.0	5.8	105.8
SD	3.4	4.4	4.1	5.5	1.1	16.1

Table 9: L1 Composition Scores of the Low Group

(total possible)	Clarity of Theme (30)	Appeal to Readers (30)	Expression (30)	Organization (30)	Knowledge of Lang. Forms (30)	Social Awareness (30)	Total (180)
Aya	16	13	15	16	19	16	95
Beni	17	17	18	15	20	16	103
Chihiro	17	14	22	11	23	18	105
Dan	17	14	16	15	19	17	98
Emi	16	14	17	13	20	20	100
Mean	16.6	14.4	17.6	14	20.2	17.4	100.2
SD	0.5	1.5	2.7	2.0	1.6	1.7	4.0

Table 10 presents total number of words/characters, sentences, and paragraphs per composition. The total number of words (in L2) ranged from 60 to 185, whereas that of characters (in L1) ranged from 323 to 579. The quantity of production also varied more in L2 than in L1. Regarding words/characters produced, a common tendency emerged at the individual writer level. The most and least productive writers in L1 also had high and low production in L2. Dan had the smallest amount of production in L1/L2, whereas Emi produced the most in L1 and the second largest output in L2 (see the L1 and L2 Writing Processes section for discussion). L1/L2 composition scores and words/characters are referred to wherever relevant in the writing processes section.

Table 10: Total Number of Characters/Words, Sentences and Paragraphs

	No. of Characters/Words L1	L2	No. of Sentences L1	L2	No. of Paragraphs L1	L2
Aya	452	185	8	12	2	2
Beni	343	115	7	6	1	3
Chihiro	543	148	10	10	1	1
Dan	323	60	9	7	1	1
Emi	579	156	18	16	1	2
Mean	448	132.8	10.4	10.2	1.2	1.8
SD	114.9	48.1	4.4	4.0	0.45	0.84

Regarding the quantity of sentences and paragraphs, there were no noticeable differences between L1 and L2. The Wilcoxon Matched-Pairs Signed Ranks tests found no significant differences on both measures. The most and least productive writers in terms of the number of sentences were the same. In both L1 and L2, generally the students did not produce much. More specifically, they wrote approximately a one-paragraph composition in both languages (see Appendixes D, E and G for low students' sample L1/L2 compositions). This finding partly confirms the finding of Nishigaki and Leishman (1998), who reported that inexperienced Japanese EFL students often wrote English compositions consisting of one extended paragraph with no introduction or conclusion. Regardless of language, they might have lacked knowledge about composition such as indentation and paragraphing.

With regard to the relation between quantity and quality, there did not seem to be any relation. However, the smallest producer in terms of words/characters, Dan, had the lowest score in L2 and the second lowest score in L1. On the other hand, the second smallest producer in L1/L2, Beni, scored the second best in both L1 and L2. The relation between quantity and quality should be further examined with a much larger number of participants.

L1 and L2 Writing Processes

(1) Total Writing Time and Prewriting Time

Table 11 reports the results of measures used for writing process analysis, total time spent and time spent prewriting. Regarding the total time spent, the mean L1 time was 25 minutes 40 seconds, and the mean L2 time was 34 minutes 28 seconds. Thus, on average, the students spent more than 8 minutes longer in L2 writing. This finding accords with those of previous studies (e.g., Hall, 1990; Silva, 1993), in which students were found to consume more time in L2 writing. As Table 11 reports, all except Dan took more total time in L2. Aya, in particular, spent more than twice as much time for L2 writing.

The prewriting time in L1 ranged from 1 minute 23 seconds to 8 minutes 27 seconds ($M=$ 3 min 44 s), whereas that in L2 ranged from 2 minutes to 5 minutes 38 seconds ($M=$ 3 min 56 s). On average, they spent slightly more mean time (12 seconds) before writing the first sentence in L2. This finding does not seem to be comparable to those of previous studies on weak writers. Raimes (1985), for example, found that the prewriting time of unskilled ESL students ranged from 45 seconds to 2 minutes 12 seconds in L2. The present participants took more prewriting time than Raimes' (1985) participants. What they did before writing the first words are examined in the Qualitative Analysis of Strategies section.

Table 11: Total Time Spent and Time Spent on Prewriting

	Total Time Spent		Time Spent on Prewriting	
	L1	L2	L1	L2
Aya	23:03	48:46	1:35	3:26
Beni	20:15	25:36	3:54	4:55
Chihiro	25:09	28:22	3:20	2:00
Dan	35:04	32:54	8:27	5:38
Emi	24:49	36:44	1:23	3:40
Mean	25:40	34:28	3:44	3:56

Note: 23:03 = minutes: seconds

(2) Quantitative Analysis of Pauses and Strategies

Table 12 presents total numbers of pauses and strategies used during pauses. The mismatch between the number of pauses and that of strategies in Table 12 derived from the fact that students mostly employed more than one strategy during pauses. As it shows, the

Table 12: Number of Pauses and Strategies in L1 and L2 Writing

	No. of Pauses		No. of Strategies	
	L1	L2	L1	L2
Aya	10	14	17	21
Beni	14	29	13	39
Chihiro	24	22	30	28
Dan	17	7	22	13
Emi	17	38	25	44
Mean	16.4	22.0	21.4	29.0
SD	5.1	12.2	6.7	12.7

students paused more in L2 ($M=22.0$) than in L1 ($M=16.4$). Similarly, they employed more strategies in L2 ($M=29.0$) than in L1 ($M=21.4$). However, the difference of the number of strategies in L1 and L2 was not found to be statistically significant; $z=-.94$, $p=.35$, nor was the difference in the number of pauses; $z=-.94$, $p=.35$ by the Wilcoxon Matched-Pairs Signed Ranks test.

Because pause time varied, a larger number of pauses does not simply imply more blocked writing. For example, Dan spent the longest time before writing the first sentence both in L1 and L2. Although his pause number in L2 was less than half of that in L1 and the smallest in the group, his pause time was lengthy and he spent more time thinking about the topic than writing about it. His small generation of words/characters probably reflected this process. He was a contemplator, and in fact he was the only student who said he would have required much more time to put his thoughts into words fully on paper. In sharp contrast, Emi paused most frequently (38 times) in L2 (see Appendix E for Emi's L1/L2 compositions). Unlike Dan, her pause time was generally short and she produced the largest number of sentences in L1/L2 without intra-sentential pauses. In either language, Emi was a fluent, spontaneous writer who wrote down whatever came to mind. In L1, she seemed to write fluently judging from the number of sentences she wrote, and she produced the largest amount of characters (recall Table 10). In fact, she described herself as "a person who writes without much thinking." In L2, she first wrote down every sentence in L1 on her draft paper, and then translated into L2. This strategy probably generated more pauses than in L1 but facilitated her production of L2 sentences. She produced the largest number of L2 sentences in the group.

In spite of such differences in their L1/L2 writing processes, Dan's and Emi's total L1 scores did not differ much (only 2 points), whereas their

Table 13: Total Number of Strategies Used[5]

		Planning				Retrieval		Generation		Verbalization			Re-reading	Others	Total
		P_P	P_L	P_O	P_C	R_P	R	G	A	T	L	L_L	E		
Aya	L1	0	5	0	2	0	0	0	0	0	0	2	8	0	17
	L2	0	6	0	1	0	0	0	1	3	0	3	7	0	21
Beni	L1	1	5	0	0	0	0	1	1	0	0	2	3	0	13
	L2	1	2	0	2	3	0	1	2	14	3	4	7	0	39
Chihiro	L1	0	4	1	1	0	0	0	1	3	1	6	12	1	30
	L2	0	6	0	1	0	0	1	1	8	1	7	3	0	28
Dan	L1	1	2	1	1	1	1	3	1	0	1	4	5	1	22
	L2	1	3	0	1	1	2	0	0	1	1	2	1	0	13
Emi	L1	0	5	0	1	1	0	1	1	5	0	3	8	0	25
	L2	0	9	0	1	4	0	0	2	16	0	9	3	0	44
Mean	L1	0.4	4.2	0.4	1.0	0.4	0.2	1.0	0.8	1.6	0.4	3.4	7.2	0.4	21.4
	L2	0.4	5.2	0	1.2	1.6	0.4	0.4	1.2	8.4	1.0	5	4.2	0	29.0

Table 14: Mean Number and Ratio of Strategies Used

	L1	L2
Planning Total	6.0 (28%)	6.8 (23.4%)
P_P (Global Planning)	0.4 (1.9%)	0.4 (1.4%)
P_L (Local Planning)	4.2 (19.6%)	5.2 (17.9%)
P_O (Idea Sorting)	0.4 (1.9%)	0 (0%)
P_C (Conclusion Planning)	1.0 (4.7%)	1.2 (4.1%)
Retrieval Total	0.6 (2.8%)	2.0 (6.9%)
R_P (Retrieving Plans)	0.4 (1.9%)	1.6 (5.5%)
R (Retrieving Information from Memory)	0.2 (0.9%)	0.4 (1.4%)
Generation Total	1.8 (8.4%)	1.6 (5.5%)
G (Spontaneous Idea Generation)	1.0 (4.7%)	0.4 (1.4%)
A (Idea Generation from the Text)	0.8 (3.7%)	1.2 (4.1%)
Verbalization Total	5.4 (25.2%)	14.4 (49.7%)
T (Verbalizing Propositions)	1.6 (7.5%)	8.4 (29.0%)
L (Refining Rhetoric)	0.4 (1.9%)	1.0 (3.4%)
L_L (Correcting Surface Forms)	3.4 (15.9%)	5.0 (17.2%)
Rereading		
E	7.2 (33.6%)	4.2 (14.5%)
Others	0.4 (1.9%)	0 (%)

total L2 scores differed by 44 points (Tables 8 and 9). The smaller quantity of Dan's output might have damaged his L2 score more than his L1 score. Or, the larger quantity of Emi's output in L2, that is, about 2.5 times that of Dan's in terms of words, helped her to score much higher in L2. Emi scored the highest, whereas Dan scored the lowest in the group.

Table 13 summarizes the results of quantitative analysis of pauses and strategies (see Appendix H for a full description of each category), whereas Table 14 presents the mean number and the ratio of each category used by the group. Tables 13 and 14 show the students mostly paused to make local plans (P_L), put their ideas into language (T), correct the surface forms (L_L), and reread (E). Because rereading (E) often co-occurred along with another category, P_L, T and L_L are the focus of the strategy analysis.[4]

(3) Qualitative Analysis of Strategies

The results of pause analysis revealed both similarities and differences between L1 and L2 writing processes. The difference between the two seems to lie in the number of pauses for the "verbalization" phase (T, L, L_L), especially T. Besides this difference, several similarities seem to be apparent between the two writing processes. In this section, similarities and differences are discussed based on the qualitative analysis of the protocol data. The discussion here is limited to the four strategies, P_L, E, L_L, and T, because the four combined accounted for as much as 76.6% in L1 and 78.6% in L2 (see Table 14).

1) Similarities between L1 and L2 Processes

As for similarities between L1 and L2 writing, all participants were found to pause to plan what to write next (P_L), reread (E), and to recall correct surface forms and/or make corrections of perceived mistakes (L_L). For example, Chihiro, before writing in both L1 and L2, paused over the opening sentence. He started to write when ideas flashed into his mind. This way of getting started seems to resemble Bereiter and Scardamalia's (1987) "knowledge-telling" model. According to the model, an immature writer takes the start-up time "to retrieve a first item of content fitting requirements of the topic and genre" (p. 13). When he retrieved the first item to write (i.e., his junior and senior high school days) in L2, Chihiro lost no time in writing it down. After writing his opening sentence "I wore salor suit when I was junior high school or high school," he paused to plan what to write next. At that point, he thought about what to connect his experience of wearing uniforms with. This pause was coded as **A** (idea generation from the text) followed by **P$_L$**. Later he paused to reread the sentence he had just written and to plan what to write next (**E** followed by **P$_L$**).

The low-level students also relied on **P$_L$** while writing in L1. They continued writing until they ran out of ideas. Aya, for example, thought of finishing when no ideas came to mind in L1, too. However, she decided to write a little more, feeling something was missing in her L1 text. She planned what to write, and she actually wrote one more sentence. Rereading the sentence, she thought about what else to write, but she did not find anything else. She reported she could not help stopping writing at that point, although she felt it would have been better to make a further assertion. Although she did not pause to put her ideas into language (T), she resorted to **P$_L$** and **E** most in L1 (recall Table 13). This way of low students' writing until they had no ideas is consistent with the "knowledge-telling" writing model (Bereiter & Scardamalia, 1987). Most low students in the present chapter seem to have approached writing following the "knowledge-telling" model rather than the "knowledge-transforming" model.

Low proficiency level students might have been preoccupied with filling in the writing space as much as possible, particularly in L2 writing. Aya, for example, actually reported she was concerned with filling in the writing space while writing in L2. She thought of stopping writing once, but instead she added one more paragraph. In fact, she asked me whether she had to write down to the bottom line on the paper just after having finished writing. Under the pressure to fill in space, it might have been characteristic of less proficient L2 writers to plan locally (P_L), make a word-, phrase- or sentence-level translation (T), reread this (E), and then plan (P_L) again until their ideas or time ran out.

The high ratios of correcting the surface forms (L_L) also showed that these low-proficiency students exercised some care concerning accuracy while writing in L1/L2 (recall Table 14). The students paused to recall correct surface forms before writing them. Alternatively, by rereading the word, phrase, clause or sentence just written, they corrected perceived mistakes in terms of accuracy at the linguistic level including spelling, Chinese characters, and grammar. As an example of the grammar correction, Chihiro shifted from past to future by adding, "will." Regarding L2 writing, the finding appears to be inconsistent with Raimes' (1985) unskilled ESL writers and Uzawa's (1996) Japanese ESL students, who did not particularly pay attention to accuracy. However, this finding is consistent with Pianko's (1979) "remedial" L1 writers, who were particularly concerned about mechanics, usage, and correct wording.

Nevertheless, it is interesting that 2 out of 5 participants (40%) also paused for global planning (P_P) before beginning to write the first sentence in L1/L2 writing (recall Table 13). Beni wrote down a similar plot plan (in which the statement of her position was followed by its supporting reasons) in L1 before writing the first sentence (see Appendix G), whereas Dan made a global plan with the *ki-shô-ten-ketsu* in mind without writing it down in notes. Interestingly, both Beni and Dan reported that they knew an opinion-stating composition starts with the statement followed by the reasons to justify the position. Dan further explained that the argument for the position would precede the counterargument, which would be followed by its confutation. Because they had not received L2 writing instruction yet, they apparently had acquired this knowledge in L1 instruction and applied it in L2 writing. This finding does not accord with that of previous research, in which only good writers tended to be concerned with overall organization (Sasaki & Hirose, 1996). Despite their awareness of organization, however, Beni's and Dan's L1/L2 organization scores were no better than other participants who did not make a global plan before writing. This finding implies that the mere presentation of the writer's position and its reasons does not necessarily produce well-organized writings (see Chapter 5 for further discussion on this matter). For probably different reasons, their use of this good writers' writing strategy did not lead to better-organized compositions in L1/L2. As her notes in Appendix G show, Beni appears to have simply jotted down her own experiences related to the given topics without the notion of persuading the expected readers to accept her views. For example, her L2 composition, in which she mostly translated her notes into L2, reflected her personal experiences such as her high school days and her brother. It is worth mentioning that Beni was aware of this. Just after she finished writing, she reflected that her personal aspects such as family background had been put forward too much and she might have got them wrong in her writing. On the other hand, in the case of Dan, his small production in L1/L2 (only 60 words long in L2; recall Table 10) did not help his argument to be fully developed.

    Students' use of common strategies in L1/L2 may reveal that they have transferred L1 writing strategies to L2 writing. Common strategy use seems to have contributed to making each participant's L1/L2 writing process similar. This finding is consistent with that of Raimes (1987), who implied that writing strategies cross languages. Raimes (1987) also suggests that L2 writers bring L1 problems, linguistic rhetorical knowledge, and strategies for L1 writing to L2 writing. Low-proficiency students in the present study appear to have brought L1 knowledge and strategy including problems to L2 writing.

2) Differences between L1 and L2 Processes

Regardless of the similarities mentioned above, differences did exist between L1 and L2 writing processes. As shown in Table 13, "verbalizing propositions"(**T**) occurred much more in L2 writing. Naturally, the process of putting ideas into language should differ between L1 and L2. For example, the participants had already put their ideas into words in L1 when they consciously hunted for corresponding L2 words. The hunt for L2 words must have been an additional process that did not subsist in the L1 process of putting ideas into words. This extra process involved in hunting for words (or constructing sentences) resulted in much higher occurrences of **T** in L2 writing. It is apparent that in L2 **T** was further extended to include translating. Nevertheless, it was difficult to distinguish **T** from translating in the present recall protocol data; thus the same category (**T**) was used for L2 in the present study.[6]

As Table 13 shows, all low students paused more for **T** in L2 than in L1. In the case of low proficiency level students, higher occurrence of **T** in L2 obviously resulted from translation problems. It was likely that they were most concerned with retrieving L2 vocabulary that corresponded to the L1 counterpart. For example, in response to the general question regarding what he was thinking of while writing in L2 that was asked immediately after he finished writing, Dan simply answered, "Words." In fact, he also reported that it cost him much time to retrieve every word in L2. Once he found an L2 word, its spelling was his next concern. For example, he changed "there" into "their" (homophones) at four places (the personal pronoun "their" was correct). Whereas he reported retrospectively having been concerned with overall organization (recall Chapter 1), he focused his attention on spelling while writing in L2. The students were fully aware of their limited range of vocabulary that prevented them from writing what they wanted to write in L2. They all reported that L2 words did not come to mind and thus they made desperate word searches. For example, in the following excerpt, Beni explained about her problem of translation:

> Me: In the middle of line 3, you were not looking at your notes much. You were pondering over something here, weren't you?
> Beni: Yes, in a way, how to write in English was . . . .
> Me: What was your problem? Was it "朝の少ない"? You have just deleted something here on line 3.
> Beni: I think I was pondering over how to write "朝の少ない時間" But the English expression did not come to mind, so well . . . .
> Me: How did you solve the problem of expressing "朝の少ない時間" in English, then?
> Beni: I wrote, "in short time" (H: What?) "in short."
> Me: "In short time." You ended up with "短い間に" (=in short time)?
> Beni: I wrote, "I wore it." (H: I see.) Well, around here I really could not put it into appropriate English expressions.

Before writing, Beni took notes, which included "朝の少ない時間" (=limited time in the morning). As she explained, her end sentence was "in short time I wore it." The above pause was coded as **T** being used. When she was stuck, Beni had already verbalized her ideas in L1 and was apparently translating the L1 "朝の少ない時間" into L2.

As Beni's protocol excerpt showed, L1 words were replaced by known L2 words within her reach. She did not have many L2 words at her disposal. This could have resulted in message reduction. By writing "in short time I wore it," what Beni attempted to mean was "I could manage to put on my school uniform even in the limited time in the morning." Beni herself was fully aware of the gap between the intended meaning and the expressed meaning, as her last utterance in the above protocol excerpt implied. Her dissatisfaction with it made her add the following adverbial clause "because I had a lot of homework so I stayed up late night." She had not written this clause previously in her L1 notes but considered "in short time I wore it" insufficient and lacking in explanation after writing them. Probably what she wanted to add by the adverbial clause was something like she did not have much time in the morning because she stayed up late to do a lot of homework and could not get up early.

L2 word searches did not always lead to reduced message as shown in Beni's case above, but to a failure (i.e., incomprehensible message). For example, Emi attempted to translate her planned L1 expression "(個性を)つぶす" (=deteriorate individuality) but did not think of an English verb that corresponded to "つぶす" (=ruin). She then rewrote her L1 notes by deleting "(個性を)つぶす" and writing "don't 生産する" (=don't create individuality) instead, producing "some of them think that to wear school uniforms don't indrect their personality" in her final L2 text. Her final expression, "don't indrect," did not convey her intended meaning (=don't create) at all. How she got a non-existent word "indrect" is difficult to uncover.

If no L2 words were found and the original ideas were not dropped, either L1 words were used or L2 words were even created on the spot.

An example of the former is found in Beni's composition, which had a Japanese verb: "反抗する their parents" (=disobey their parents) (see Appendix G). She actually attempted to write an English expression for "反抗期" (=the period of rebelliousness), but she had to paraphrase it. The latter example is found in one of Dan's sentences, "I'm stand place is disagree school uniform," which was probably derived from the direct transposition of the L1 sentence meaning "My position is against school uniforms." When he could not hit on "position," "stand place," presumably a combination of Chinese characters 立 (=stand) and 場 (=place) was his own coinage.

In addition to L2 vocabulary, L2 syntactic structures did not come automatically, either. Students sometimes put familiar English words in a more L1-like order, although they did not do so to the extent which they produced the L1 order of SOV. Thus, the main sentence structure was English, but it contained Japanese flavor. For example, Chihiro wrote, "I think young person need other thinking things," which has a pre-modification structure. This was intended to mean, "I think young people should think of things other than clothing" (in which the original pre-modified phrase takes a post-modification structure). Chihiro's phrase "other thinking things" showed that he passed through a word-for-word translation process from L1 to L2; "他の" (=other), "考える" (=thinking), and "こと" (=things). Similarly, Emi wrote "毎朝大変である" in her notes and then wrote "So I am hard every morning," by which she meant, "Because I don't wear a school uniform any more, I find it hard to choose what to wear every morning."

Although these L2 sentences were to a certain degree comprehensible, many L2 sentences were not. For example, Aya's sentence, "If students wear the freedom clothes at school, between student will exist on the composition," was a case in point. In this example, although "the freedom clothes" in the adverbial clause could be interpreted as "free clothing," the main clause was difficult to interpret. According to Aya's retrospective reports, it was meant to be that "disparity will result among students." Although her wrong choice of the noun "composition" makes the meaning unclear, Aya obviously made a word-for-word translation from an L1 clause like "生徒間に格差が存在するようになる" (=Among students will be disparity) into the L2 counterpart. Just like Emi and Chihiro above, Aya made an overall English sentence structure but integrated Japanese order into the English structure. These examples seem to show that these lower proficiency level students depended on verbatim translation, at a small unit like the word level, from L1 to L2. For this reason, they attended to local words, rather than to syntactical structures while writing in L2.

Thus, it was more likely for low-proficiency students to resort extensively to L1 when they searched for ideas or plans, and then to translate into L2. These processes resulted in pausing to replace L1 words with L2 counterparts. As discussed above, Emi wrote L1 at a sentence level before translating it into L2. This cyclical process of L1-L2 translation probably helped to produce the highest occurrence of T in Emi's L2 writing among the group (recall Table 13). Her use of detailed notes in L1 during L2 writing is worth mentioning especially because she wrote no notes while she was writing in L1. Similarly, Aya, who did not write any notes in L1 writing, wrote two complete sentences in L1 before starting to write in L2. She struggled with translating them into L2 and decided to stop writing notes in L1 because she felt it much harder to replace an L1 sentence with an L2 counterpart. According to her report, she then started to write directly in L2 and even wrote one L2 sentence in notes during L2 writing. This complex process probably made her take twice as much writing time in L2 writing (recall Table 11). Nevertheless, their use of notes may have helped facilitate their L2 production. Aya produced the largest number of words, and Emi produced the second largest in the low group (recall Table 10). In contrast, Chihiro did not write any notes before writing his L2 text. Nevertheless, he reported that he thought about what to write in L1 but it took him time to translate into L2. For example, he wondered how to translate "服" (=clothes) and "中高生" (=junior and senior high school students). In the latter case, he ended up with the phrase "young person," thus substituting the troubling expression with superordinate words.

Message modification or reduction was also made beyond a phrase, clause, or sentence level. Aya testified about such a message reduction case. She wrote, "When the student becomes adult, there will be good memory." After writing her L2 text, she explained what she had meant by this sentence was something like, "In the future, the students feel nostalgic about the days when they wore school uniforms. Such days will make good memories on them. Thus, they have such valuable experience by wearing uniforms." Nevertheless, as she reflected, these sentences did not come out when she was writing in L2.

As exemplified above, the lower-proficiency students were particularly concerned with processes involving putting generated content into English, adapting it to their L2 proficiency level sufficient to expressing it. That is, they had not reached an L2 proficiency level or accumulated L2 writing experience sufficient for direct writing in L2. The participants in this chapter were conscious of having engaged in message abandonment, message modification or reduction due to their limited L2 proficiency. Thus, the findings imply that limited knowledge and/or control of L2 impeded these students' L2 writing. On the other hand, they also resorted to compensatory strategies to make up for their limited L2 proficiency. First, the low-proficiency students in the present study had a tendency to engage a small linguistic unit (such as a word-for-word) translation from L1 to L2. They seemed to use direct translation as a compensatory strategy. A notable case was Emi, who scored the highest in the group. Second, some students were motivated to fill out the writing space. For example, Emi reported having written down anything she could manage to verbalize in L2. After writing a sentence, "In the company, worker are wearing uniforms," she thought of increasing the number of sentences and thus decided to write about herself. According to her retrospective report, the next sentence, "I'm also wearing uniform in my company," soon came out because it was simple (see Appendix E). Presumably the sentence was easily formulated because it had a syntactic structure and vocabulary similar to those used in the previous sentence, "In the company, worker are wearing uniforms." Thus, for Emi, using the parallel structure and vocabulary items (i.e., be-verb, wearing uniform, in company) may be not only a compensatory strategy, but also a facilitative strategy to create a large amount of production. This example demonstrates that students can resort to repetition to compensate for their limited ability under the pressure to fill out the writing space. In so doing, they run the risk of using repetitions and parallel structures, which may result in producing compositions with poor organization and underdeveloped argument. Nevertheless, inexperienced L2 student-writers need more opportunities in L2 to write what they intend to write.

Chapter 3
L1 and L2 Writing Processes of High L2 Proficiency Level Students

In Chapter 2, I investigated L1/L2 writing processes of low English proficiency level Japanese EFL students and found not only similarities but also differences between L1 and L2 writing processes within an individual student. More specifically, the results revealed that in both L1 and L2 the students paused mostly to do local planning (i.e., planning what to write next), put their ideas into language, correct the surface forms and reread. Thus, like Uzawa's (1996) inexpert Japanese participants, most students appear to have employed the "what next strategy" (Bereiter & Scardamalia, 1987). Unlike Uzawa's writers, however, these students exercised some care concerning accuracy while writing in L1/L2. This discrepancy found between the two studies can be attributed to one writing condition Uzawa (1996) assigned to her tasks, that is, writing a first draft, not a final one. As for the difference between L1 and L2 writing processes found in Chapter 2, the low students tended to pause more in L2 to put their ideas into language by attempting to do lexical retrieval while accommodating their restricted range of vocabulary. By doing so, they engaged in message abandonment, modification or reduction due to their limited L2 proficiency. These verbalization processes should be easier for higher proficiency or more experienced L2 students. To ascertain whether students pause less to put their ideas into L2 as their proficiency develops and to examine the extent to which their L2 writing processes differ from those of L1, a comparative study of L1/L2 writing processes of advanced EFL students needs to be undertaken.

Research Questions

The present chapter focuses on how high-proficiency students' L2 writing processes differ from those of L1 using a within-subject design.[1] It explores the following questions:

Are there differences in high proficiency level Japanese EFL students' processes of L1 and L2 writing? If so, how and to what extent do their L2 writing processes differ from their L1 writing processes?

As in Chapter 2, process analysis was done both quantitatively and qualitatively, and process analysis was complemented by product analysis.

Method

Participants

As in Chapter 1, 6 Japanese university students comprised the same high group. Except for 1 graduate student, the participants were solicited from among 50 third-year students majoring in British and American Studies in a Japanese university in 1997, based on their CELT scores (see Table 1). Making reference to the CELT scores of the good writer group (mean total score = 201.2) in a previous study (Sasaki & Hirose, 1996), those students with a CELT total score of over 200 were asked if they could participate in my research outside class, and they were financially compensated for their time. Judging from their CELT scores, the participants' L2 proficiency level was high-intermediate to advanced (CELT M = 240.3, SD = 14.3, range = 216 to 260). Thus, the present participants' L2 level was higher than that of the good writer group in the previous study (Sasaki & Hirose, 1996), and they could be characterized as advanced Japanese EFL students.

The participants had studied English for at least 8 years through the Japanese school system, and they had taken at least 1 year-long English writing course at university. In addition to having received an English writing course per se, all students had some academic writing experience in English (writing assignments or short papers for other courses), which is not usually the case with most Japanese EFL university students. One of the participants, in particular, had studied English in a community college in the U.S. for 2 years, and had taken English writing courses there. Apart from this student's experience studying abroad, the participants did not differ very much in terms of age, academic major, previous educational background in L1/L2, and L2 proficiency level.

The data were collected and analyzed in exactly the same way as explained in Chapter 2, thus the explanation is omitted in the present chapter.

Results and Discussion

L1 and L2 Writing Products

Tables 15 and 16 show each participant's L2 and L1 composition scores, respectively. The total score mean was 158.8 (79.4%) in L2 and 128.5 (71.4%) in L1. Their L2 writing scores appeared better than those of

L1. In terms of percent, 4 out of 6 participants actually had better scores in L2. In particular, Jiro's L2 score (88.5%) was much better than his L1 score (65%). However, it is problematic to claim that his L2 writing ability was better than that of his L1. The L1/L2 scores should not be compared directly for the same writer. Different writing scales were used to measure students' L1 and L2 writing abilities respectively, and readers' expectations are likely to be different in evaluating L1 and L2 compositions.

According to the interpretive guide for placement into ESL writing skill levels (Hughey et al., 1983), 79.4 was considered within the "Low Advanced" level at university, and "writers with scores 75 to 80 and above usually enter regular English classes" (Hughey et al., 1983, p. 235) in a U.S. university. Regarding L1 writing scores, they were considered "good" writers (Sasaki & Hirose, 1999). Thus, they could be regarded as good, if not excellent, writers in both L1 and L2. Another thing to be noted regarding L1/L2 compositions was that the standard deviations (*SD*s) of L2 were generally larger than those of L1. For example, compare the *SD* of language use in L2 (7.5) with that of expression in L1 (0.4). These findings suggest that there were greater variations in L2 scores than in L1 scores.

Table 15: L2 Composition Scores of the High Group

(total possible)	Content (60)	Organization (40)	Vocabulary (40)	Lang. Use (50)	Mechanics (10)	Total (200)
Fumi	47	29	31	26	8	141
Ginko	42	25	26	29	9	131
Hikari	53	34	35	37	9	168
Ichiro	52	37	33	43	8	173
Jiro	57	36	32	43	9	177
Ken	49	33	30	42	9	163
Mean	50.0	32.3	31.2	36.7	8.7	158.8
SD	5.2	4.5	3.1	7.5	0.5	18.6

Table 16: L1 Composition Scores of the High Group

(total possible)	Clarity of Theme (30)	Appeal to Readers (30)	Expression (30)	Organization (30)	Knowledge of Lang. Forms (30)	Social Awareness (30)	Total (180)
Fumi	25	23	21	24	25	22	140
Ginko	20	18	21	22	26	19	126
Hikari	18	20	22	20	26	21	127
Ichiro	20	20	21	21	26	21	129
Jiro	19	18	21	18	19	22	117
Ken	21	21	21	25	24	20	132
Mean	20.5	20.0	21.2	21.7	24.3	20.8	128.5
SD	2.4	1.9	0.4	2.6	2.7	1.2	7.6

This is consistent with that of lower proficiency level students (recall Chapter 2). L1/L2 composition scores are referred to whenever relevant in the processes section.

Table 17 presents the total number of words/characters, sentences and paragraphs per composition. The total number of words (in L2) ranged from 105 to 228,[2] whereas that of characters (in L1) ranged from 463 to 846. The numbers of words/characters produced show that there were wide variations in both L1 and L2, and the rankings from the least to most

Table 17: Total Number of Characters/Words, Sentences and Paragraphs

	No. of Characters/Words		No. of Sentences		No. of Paragraphs	
	L1	L2	L1	L2	L1	L2
Fumi	614	176	13	17	4	6
Ginko	548	164	13	15	4	3
Hikari	463	105	9	7	3	2
Ichiro	608	228	11	15	4	4
Jiro	846	173	13	9	3	4
Ken	580	162	13	11	4	3
Mean	609.8	168	12	12.3	3.7	3.7
SD	128.1	39.3	1.7	1.6	0.2	0.6

productive in L1 almost never corresponded one-to-one with the rankings in L2. For example, the most productive L1 and L2 writers were not the same, although note that in both L1 and L2, the most productive writers produced twice as much as the least productive writer. There were, however, two consistent cases. The least productive writer in L1, Hikari, was also the least productive in L2, and Fumi was the second most productive writer in both L1 and L2.

Regarding the number of sentences and paragraphs, there were no noticeable differences between L1 and L2. It is also noteworthy that all L1/L2 compositions consisted of indented recognizable paragraphs (see Appendixes B and C for sample high students' L1/L2 compositions). Unlike the low students, the high students all indented the first line of a paragraph in L1/L2. In Japanese, it is customary to leave one space, not five or seven spaces as in English, in indentation. The students all appear to have had a sense of paragraphing conventions in both L1 and L2. This observation does not accord with those of previous studies that examined English compositions written by Japanese EFL students. Nishigaki and Leishman (1998), for example, found that these compositions were either one extended paragraph or body paragraph without introduction or conclusion.[3] Furthermore, Okabe (1983) mentioned, "Due to the lack of the paragraph sense on the part of the Japanese, however, I find it difficult, or almost impossible, as an instructor of English and communication, to teach Japanese students of English to write a coherent English paragraph" (p. 30).

The possession of the paragraph sense in L1 might have helped the participants of the present study to make paragraphs in L2, too. However, it has been argued that an English paragraph is different from the Japanese counterpart in the sense that English requires more coherence and unity within a paragraph (e.g., Kinoshita, 1990; Okabe, 1983).

From the writers' viewpoints, the present participants demonstrated that making paragraphs in English involved different processes from those in making Japanese paragraphs, and English paragraphs were not so difficult to form as expected by previous research. After completing both L1 and L2 compositions, Jiro reported that he felt it was harder to make paragraphs in Japanese. Furthermore, Hikari, who made three paragraphs in L1 (see Appendix C), actually started writing a sentence at the end of a previous paragraph, erased it, and then indented to start a new paragraph with it, to produce the second and third paragraphs. In L2, in contrast, she did not take such an approach to paragraphing. These findings suggest that paragraphing in Japanese can be harder for advanced Japanese students than paragraphing in English. Therefore, despite the common belief that English paragraphs are difficult for Japanese students to form, they may be easier to make when students have reached a certain L2 writing ability level. This speculation should be investigated in a further study.

Regarding L1 and L2 compositions, it should be also noted that quantity (measured in terms of the number of words/characters) did not seem to be directly related to quality (reflected in composition scores; see Tables 15 and 16). Hikari, as discussed above, had the smallest production in L1/L2. But the small quantity of her output did not seem to damage her L1/L2 scores much. In contrast to Hikari, Jiro produced the largest number of characters, but he received the lowest L1 score in the group.

L1 and L2 Writing Processes

(1) Total Writing Time and Prewriting Time

Table 18 presents the results of measures used for process analysis; total time spent and time spent on prewriting. Regarding the total time spent, the mean L1 time was 31 minutes 46 seconds, and the mean L2 time was 31 minutes 55 seconds. As a group, they spent only slightly more mean time (9 seconds) in L2. This finding is not comparable to those of previous studies (e.g., Hall, 1990), where students took more writing time in L2.

As Table 18 reports, half of the present participants took more time writing in L2 than in L1. However, at an individual level there were no significant differences between L1 and L2 except for the following two cases. Ginko took more than 8 minutes longer in L2 than in L1. On the other hand, Jiro consumed more than 9 minutes longer time in L1. Thus, in the present study, the students' L1 and L2 total writing time did not differ much, but there were also variations within some students. The results should be interpreted with some caution because the topics were different.[4]

Table 18: Total Time Spent and Time Spent on Prewriting

| | Total Time Spent | | Time Spent on Prewriting | |
	L1	L2	L1	L2
Fumi	42:10	41:48	5:53	6:51
Ginko	32:09	40:30	6:32	3:40
Hikari	29:08	30:18	1:40	1:35
Ichiro	33:42	32:22	3:10	4:40
Jiro	31:34	22:26	4:37	5:41
Ken	21:55	24:07	3:20	4:53
Mean	31:46	31:55	4:12	4:33

Note: 42:10 = minutes: seconds

The prewriting time in L1 ranged from 1 minute 40 seconds to 6 minutes 32 seconds (M = 4 min 12 s), whereas that in L2 ranged from 1 minute 35 seconds to 6 minutes 51 seconds (M = 4 min 33 s). As a group, they spent slightly more (21 seconds) time on prewriting in L2. Four students (66.7%) spent more time on prewriting in L2. Exceptionally, Ginko consumed about half as much prewriting time in L2 as in L1; however, it took her more than 8 minutes longer to complete the L2 task. Thus, her shorter prewriting time was complemented by much longer writing time in L2. These contrastive findings of Ginko's total writing and prewriting times in L1/L2 writing can be partly explained by the notes she made before writing the first sentence in relation to compositions (see Appendix F). In her notes for L1 composition, she stated her position on top, followed by reasons. Her L1 composition had exactly the same content in the same order. In contrast, in her notes for L2 composition, she made a list of her thoughts or ideas for both positions. What the students did before writing the first words will be further examined in the Qualitative Analysis of Strategies section.

The results of these time measures implied they had no noticeable relation with quantity (measured in the number of words/characters; see Table 17) or quality (reflected in composition scores; see Tables 15 and 16). Instead the results seem to reveal variations both among the students and within students. For example, Fumi took the most writing time both in L1 and L2, but she did not have the largest production in L1/L2. Similarly, Ken spent the least writing time in L1 (about half as much time as Fumi), but his total number of characters was not the smallest. Thus, total time spent was not directly related to quantity. The time spent was not related to quality either, especially in Jiro's case. He took more than 9 minutes longer writing time in L1 than in L2, and he consumed the least writing time in L2. Nevertheless, he received the worst L1 and the best L2 score in the group (see Tables 15 and 16). Because he had the largest production in L1, it is clear that neither the time spent nor the quantity was related to quality.

(2) Quantitative Analysis of Pauses and Strategies

Table 19 shows total numbers of pauses and strategies used during pauses. The students paused more in L2 ($M=19.5$) than in L1 ($M=14.2$), except Ichiro. Similarly, they employed more strategies in L2 ($M=34.3$) than in L1 ($M=29.5$). However, the difference in the number of strategies in L1 and L2 was not found to be statistically significant: $z=-.94$, $p=.35$; nor was the difference in the number of pauses: $z=-1.8$, $p=.07$ by the Wilcoxon Matched-Pairs Signed Ranks test. The present study did not find pauses to be significantly more frequent in L2, unlike previous studies as reviewed by Silva (1993).

Table 19: Number of Pauses and Strategies in L1 and L2 Writing

	No. of Pauses L1	L2	No. of Strategies L1	L2
Fumi	14	21	28	40
Ginko	11	18	30	40
Hikari	12	23	34	46
Ichiro	21	17	44	31
Jiro	11	21	19	26
Ken	16	17	22	22
Mean	14.2	19.5	29.5	34.2
SD	3.9	2.5	8.9	9.3

Table 20 presents the results of detailed quantitative analysis of pauses and strategies (recall Appendix H for the coding categories and examples), whereas Table 21 reports the ratios of each strategy used. The participants paused mostly to reread (**E**), put their ideas into language (**T**), refine expressions rhetorically (**L**), or to recall correct surface forms and/or make corrections of perceived mistakes (**L_L**) regardless of language. Regarding rereading (**E**), it often co-occurred with another

Table 20: Total Number of Strategies Used

		Planning				Retrieval		Generation		Verbalization					Rereading	Others	Total
		Pp	P_L	P_O	P_C	R_p	R	G	A	T	L	L_L	L_C	F	E		
Fumi	L1	1	3	0	2	0	1	0	3	1	6	1	0	0	10	0	28
	L2	1	3	3	2	2	0	0	2	7	7	6	1	0	6	0	40
Ginko	L1	1	0	1	2	1	2	0	0	2	3	6	0	0	12	0	30
	L2	1	0	1	2	2	0	0	0	7	7	6	0	0	13	1	40
Hikari	L1	1	1	0	1	2	0	0	0	3	5	2	3	3	13	0	34
	L2	1	0	0	2	1	0	0	0	2	8	8	0	0	18	6	46
Ichiro	L1	1	5	2	2	2	3	3	2	5	0	2	2	1	14	0	44
	L2	1	3	1	1	2	0	1	1	4	4	3	1	1	8	0	31
Jiro	L1	1	2	1	1	1	1	0	0	1	3	2	1	0	5	0	19
	L2	1	1	0	1	0	0	0	2	9	3	3	2	0	2	2	26
Ken	L1	1	0	0	1	0	0	0	0	8	1	3	0	0	7	1	22
	L2	1	1	0	2	1	1	1	1	3	1	0	1	0	5	4	22
Mean	L1	1	1.8	0.7	1.5	1.0	1.2	0.5	0.8	3.3	3	2.7	1.0	0.7	10.2	0.2	29.5
	L2	1	1.3	0.8	1.7	1.3	0.2	0.3	1.0	5.3	5	4.3	0.8	0.2	8.7	2.2	34.3

Table 21: Mean Number and Ratio of Strategies Used

	L1	L2
Planning Total	5.0 (16.9%)	4.8 (14.0%)
P_P (Global Planning)	1.0 (3.4%)	1.0 (2.9%)
P_L (Local Planning)	1.8 (6.1%)	1.3 (3.8%)
P_O (Idea Sorting)	0.7 (2.4%)	0.8 (2.3%)
P_C (Conclusion Planning)	1.5 (5.1%)	1.7 (5.0%)
Retrieval Total	2.2 (7.5%)	1.5 (4.4%)
R_p (Retrieving Plans)	1.0 (3.4%)	1.3 (3.8%)
R (Retrieving Information from Memory)	1.2 (4.1%)	0.2 (0.6%)
Generation Total	1.3 (4.4%)	1.3 (3.8%)
G (Spontaneous Idea Generation)	0.5 (1.7%)	0.3 (0.9%)
A (Idea Generation from the Text)	0.8 (2.7%)	1.0 (2.9%)
Verbalization Total	10.7 (36.3%)	15.6 (45.5%)
T (Verbalizing Propositions)	3.3 (11.2%)	5.3 (15.5%)
L (Refining Rhetoric)	3.0 (10.2%)	5.0 (14.6%)
L_L (Correcting Surface Forms)	2.7 (9.2%)	4.3 (12.5%)
L_C (Reader Consciousness)	1.0 (3.4%)	0.8 (2.3%)
F (Knowledge about Composition)	0.7 (2.4%)	0.2 (0.6%)
Rereading		
E	10.2 (34.6%)	8.7 (25.4%)
Others	0.2 (0.7%)	2.2 (6.4%)

strategy such as **L** or **L**_**L** (see the Qualitative Analysis of Strategies section for further discussion of co-occurrence). In the following excerpt, for example, Fumi reported that she had read what was written down so far to recall/devise refined expressions to more exactly fit her intended meaning. The pause was categorized as two strategies, **E** (rereading) and **L** (refining rhetoric), being used.

> Me: Are you reading the sentences here?
> Fumi: Yes, I was trying to . . . I wrote down "経済" (=economy) around here, but I thought this was kind of an exaggeration, and "市場経済" (=market economy). . . .
> Me: You wrote "市場経済"?
> Fumi: Yes.
> Me: You changed it to "市場経済."
> Fumi: I changed it to "市場経済."
> Me: At first, you wrote "経済" but here "市場経済."
> Fumi: I thought "経済" was too broad because only sales went up in a department store or like that. This way I thought I could narrow down the meaning.

Next to **E**, "verbalizing propositions" (**T**) was most frequently used in both L1 and L2. The next interview portion illustrates that Hikari had difficulty expressing "中高生" (=junior and senior high school students) in English. It shows that she was making a lexical selection out of several candidates, taking natural wording and the reader into consideration.

> Hikari: I thought I had to write either "junior or high school students" or "students of high school" or something like that.
> Me: You mean you were wondering how to express it.

> Hikari: I was wondering which expression is natural, or which is easier to read.
> Me: You were thinking about that here.
> Hikari: I actually wrote again and again.
> Me: You were having a hard time. So you wrote and erased these many times?
> Hikari: Right. I feel I spent an awful lot of time getting the right expression.

On the final product, Hikari chose "junior high or high school students." As discussed in the previous chapter, Chihiro, a low student, also had difficulty writing "中高生" in L2, and wrote "young person" in the end.

This type of difficulty in putting ideas into language was also found at the syntactic level. In the following excerpt, Ginko was talking about such a case.

> Me: You stopped writing here.
> Ginko: Probably here I was wondering what kind of sentence form to use.
> Me: What do you mean by "sentence form"?
> Ginko: (In the finished composition) I have this sentence; "there are no uniforms." I was thinking of how to express my thoughts (i.e., it's better not to have uniforms) into a sentence form. I mean either something like "there are no uniforms" or something like "they don't wear uniforms."

Similar linguistic selection was also made in L1 writing. The process of putting ideas into language may differ between L1 and L2, because L2 writers might have already put their ideas into L1 when they hunt for L2 words. As discussed in Chapter 2, in L2 **T** may be further extended to include translating, or translation should have a separate entry per se. However, the same category (**T**) was used for L2 in this study because it was considered difficult to distinguish between translating into L2 and putting ideas into language clearly especially in the case of high-proficiency students. In their L2 writing protocols, very few participants used words like "translate" or "translation" when explaining what they did during pauses. This, however, does not mean they did no translations from L1 to L2 (see the Differences between L1 and L2 Processes section for further discussion of L1 use in L2 writing).

Table 22 shows that the rank order of the four most frequently employed strategies (**E→T→L→L$_L$**) was exactly the same in both L1 and L2 writing. The mean ratios of the verbalization strategies **T**, **L** and **L$_L$** were slightly higher in L2. The mean total ratios of the verbalization-related strategies were 37.8% and 52% in L1 and L2, respectively. However, the differences in the numbers of these strategies used in L1 and L2 were not statistically significant. Thus, the results of quantitative analysis showed that advanced EFL students' L2 writing processes were not significantly different from those of L1. In the next section, the results of the quantitative analysis are complemented by the qualitative analysis of strategy use.

Table 22: The Four Highest Ratios of Strategies Used

L1		L2	
(1) **E** (Rereading)	34.6%	(1) **E** (Rereading)	25.4%
(2) **T** (Verbalizing Propositions)	11.2%	(2) **T** (Verbalizing Propositions)	15.5%
(3) **L** (Refining Rhetoric)	10.2%	(3) **L** (Refining Rhetoric)	14.6%
(4) **L$_L$** (Correcting Surface Forms)	9.2%	(4) **L$_L$** (Correcting Surface Forms)	12.5%

(3) Qualitative Analysis of Strategies

The quantitative analysis of writing process has found that advanced Japanese EFL students did not differ much in any of the measures examined in the present study: quantity (total number of words/characters, sentences, and paragraphs), total time of writing, prewriting time, and their use of strategies during pauses in both L1 and L2 writing. In this section, participant protocol data are analyzed qualitatively. I limit my discussion to the three types of strategies—verbalization-related strategies, rereading and planning—because they constituted the majority of strategies used (the three categories combined accounted for as much as 88.8% in L1 and 90.5% in L2, see Table 21).

1) Similarities between L1 and L2 Processes

In brief, high-proficiency students' L1/L2 writing process bore resemblance to the depiction of the "knowledge-transforming" model (Bereiter & Scardamalia, 1987). They had concerns over both content (i.e., what to write) and rhetorical aspects of text under construction (i.e., how to write), which interacted bidirectionally in writing. In L2, for example, Fumi first made a global plan and then thought about how to express her position in the first sentence. After stating her position, she thought of mentioning the opposite position. Because she wanted to turn to the opposite opinion, she reported having pondered over a transition word by which to connect to the previous sentence. She thought about writing reasons to support the opposite position partially and then negating it in order to proceed to justifying her own position. However, she decided not to do so, and instead she expressed her position again. Her first paragraph was as follows:

> I think it is necessary for high school students to wear their school uniforms. Of course, to respect their individuality by

wearing their private clothes is also very important. But I take this side that students wear their uniforms. The reasons as follow.

Initially she thought she had to argue against the opposite position to make her case, which shows that she possessed the knowledge about argumentation by producing evidence against the opposite position. She actually thought of the evidence to present but instead geared to justifying her position with supporting reasons. In the rest of her composition, she drew her attention to what the reasons were and how to effectively present them in text.

In both L1 and L2, the students used rereading (**E**) most frequently, and it was characteristic of **E** to co-occur with such verbalization-related strategies as **T**, **L** or **L$_L$**. Thus, the co-occurrence of **E** and verbalization-related strategies is the focus of this section. Apart from this type of co-occurrence, there were two findings that need to be noted related to **E**. First, unlike inexperienced writers (Bereiter & Scardamalia, 1987), the present participants did not pause at the end of a sentence to reread or to think of what to write next [local planning (**P$_L$**) in the present study]. Second, like good writers in the previous studies who reread and revised after they finished (e.g., Hirose & Sasaki, 1994), 4 students (66.7%) reread the L1/L2 compositions after they finished writing them.

The high co-occurrence of **E** with verbalization-related strategies can be explained in several ways. First, as their use of verbalization-related strategies implied, the students had concerns or uncertainty over their language choice (i.e., whether the expression would really fit the intention or convey the intended meaning to the reader). This process the high-proficiency students resorted to seems to correspond to what Cumming (1990) calls "metalinguistic and ideational thinking," that is, thinking about language use and the intended meaning concurrently. Cumming (1990) found that this concurrent thinking of both language use and gist was characteristic of participants with higher-level writing expertise, rather than lower-level expertise in his study. The findings of the present study seem to give support to his findings.

As exemplified in the occurrences of **L**, the high students had concerns for refining the expressions made to match their intentions. Less frequently, they also showed their concerns for grammar or spelling accuracy and employed **L_L**. These concerns partly led them to reread. Second, as they all made global plans before writing, these plans seemed to play a monitoring function while writing. The students all reported they wrote mostly as they had planned, especially in L2. Third, the timed writing conditions, just as in a test-taking situation, were likely to impede creative processes of writing and might have pushed them to reread more while writing. It is of interest in this context that 2 students in the present chapter reread only while writing but did not reread after they finished writing. Another possible explanation of their rereading while writing was their awareness of coherence and the reader. They wanted to make coherent compositions understandable and persuasive to the reader (**L_C**).

These four aspects of **E** are discussed by taking Hikari's rereading as a representative example. Hikari's protocols provided many cases of rereading at various linguistic levels. She was the most frequent user of **E** in L2 and the second most frequent user in L1 (recall Table 20). Nevertheless, she did not read the whole text after she finished writing in either L1 or L2. Although she consumed the least prewriting time in L1/L2 (recall Table 18), she made a mental plan of both overall organization and content. Her absence of notes in the planning stage probably meant she required less prewriting time than other participants. Her total writing time was not the shortest in L1/L2 (Table 18). While writing, she often reread at phrase-, clause-, or sentence-level and made either grammatical or spelling corrections (L_L) or undertook rhetorical refinement (L). In fact, she employed L_L and L most frequently in L2 (Table 20). By rereading her text under construction, it is likely that she monitored her text production. She had completed revision at these levels when she finished writing and did not need to reread the whole text once it was completed. While writing in L1/L2, she later reported that she had been concerned mainly with two things: (a) whether the composition being produced was coherent, and (b) whether it was going to be understood by and convincing to the reader. The other students' protocols also revealed that they were concerned with coherence and were conscious of the reader. Their attention to coherence and the reader while writing might have pushed them to reread while writing, especially given the timed writing tasks.

Next most frequently after verbalization and rereading (E), students employed planning strategies (recall Table 21). The participants all did global planning (P_P) and conclusion planning (P_C) in L1/L2. They planned overall organization before writing the very first word. While writing, however, they did not resort to local planning (P_L) much in either language. P_P, rather than P_L, appeared to drive their writing processes. This finding is consistent with those of previous studies on good writers' writing strategies (e.g., Hirose & Sasaki, 1994), whereas it is inconsistent with those of weak writers' strategies (e.g., Uzawa, 1996). Furthermore, the high students all planned their conclusions either before writing *both* the final paragraph and the final sentence (or clause) or before writing one or the other of these. Typically, rereading (E) the text constructed so far almost always preceded P_C. The students were fully aware of making concluding remarks in the final paragraph or sentence.

2) Differences between L1 and L2 Processes

As reported in Table 21, the students made the most frequent use of verbalization-related strategies in L1/L2. For example, Fumi, Ginko, and Jiro resorted to "verbalizing propositions" (**T**) many more times in L2, and Hikari and Ichiro used it one time less than in L1. Ken was exceptional because he used it more than twice as much in L1 (recall Table 20). He first wrote the L1 composition and explained in his verbal report that he had generally paused to make word selections. His report accounts for his most frequent use of **T** (8 times) during writing in L1. Interestingly, however, just after he finished writing the L2 composition, he reported, "Compared with writing in L1, I've got the impression that attention to word choice was stronger in L2." He then continued that in L1 he managed to write without thinking much whether or not the words he chose were really okay. Although at the quantitative level he used **T** much less in L2, his introspective report implied that he made more conscious, time-consuming word choices in L2. Similarly, after she finished L1/L2 writing, Ginko said, "I found it easier to write in L1 because I was able to use the words I hit upon, intact." In this context, recall Hikari who reported having "spent an awful lot of time" getting the most appropriate expression (i.e., "junior high or senior high school students") quoted above. These students' accounts show evidence that they did not have the resonance of words in English; that is, they did not know whether the chosen words resonated the intended meaning (Arndt, 1987; Leki, 1992). Lack of such resonance probably made them pay more attention to word choice in L2.

Because pause time lengths were not measured in the present analysis, it was not possible to examine whether the students actually took more time verbalizing their thoughts per pause. However, it can be speculated that students consumed more time in making lexical choices in

L2, or at least that making such choices required more attention from them. These advanced L2 students paid attention to word choice in both L1 and L2, but they perceived greater difficulty with lexical choices while writing in L2. Advanced students' attention to words while writing in L2 appears to be consistent with the results of Cumming (1989), who found that expert L2 writers characteristically displayed concerns for word choice.

The difficulty involved in L2 vocabulary search was also attested to by other students such as Jiro. Immediately after he finished writing, he was asked the following questions to examine the extent to which his planning at the time of writing the first word matched his actual writing.

> Me: Did you write what you planned to write at the beginning?
> Jiro: Yes. I wrote roughly the same as my initial plan went.
> Me: So do you mean the final content was roughly the same as the content you planned?
> Jiro: Yes, that's right.
> Me: What were you thinking when you were writing?
> Jiro: Mmm. That was probably, if I write in Japanese probably it goes like this, or what I want to write in English. Several things came to my mind simultaneously. Then....
> Me: Then?
> Jiro: I was thinking I want to write this way in English, and words, several words stayed blank, I mean the words I did not know.
> Me: Do you mean English words?
> Jiro: Yes.
> Me: You were thinking, but some English words did not surface.

In the subsequent interview, Jiro gave two Japanese words on which he got stuck while writing in L2. He said he had a long pause at these times, when he was occupied with lexical searches for English words that fit his intended meaning.

Regarding their frequent use of such verbalization-related strategies as **T** and **L** (refining expressions rhetorically), it should also be noted that these advanced students generated alternative choices and attempted to choose the most appropriate expression based on their intuitions, although in L2 they were not always sure if they had made the right choice or not. They were concerned with appropriateness of words or structures in L1/L2. This finding seems to accord with one of the good writers' strategies Cohen (1990) characterized as follows: "expert writers indulge in a memory search and subsequent analysis of the material retrieved. The writers generate alternative language choices, assess their qualities, and choose among them according to the context and their intentions" (p. 108).

Finally, as also mentioned in Chapter 1, half of the high students (Fumi, Jiro, and Ken) reported they made more detailed plans before writing L2 compositions, and they actually took more prewriting time in L2 (recall Table 18). They appeared to make more complete plans to compensate for their L2 linguistic limitation and to facilitate their L2 writing. Jiro and Ken did not write any notes, whereas Fumi made notes in both L1 and L2 writing. Not only the quantity of the notes written but also the functions they served were different. In L2 writing, Fumi wrote more notes and more frequently. More specifically, she made notes for global planning before writing the first sentence and also while writing probably for local planning or rehearsing. These high-proficiency students did more detailed global planning before writing in L2, and the plans seemed to guide the whole writing processes in a relatively controlled way. This compensatory strategy may have helped free them from generating and organizing ideas while writing. Instead, they were able to concentrate on language production activities such as making vocabulary choices while writing in L2. This strategy seemed to play a facilitative role for L2 writing.

Differently from those high students who made more detailed planning for L2, one high student, Ginko, appeared to be more flexible with her L2 writing. For both compositions, she prepared the notes in L1 before writing the first sentence and then wrote based on the notes. Nevertheless, the notes for L1/L2 compositions were composed in a different way (see Appendix F for Ginko's notes). As discussed above, she took the longest, and much more prewriting time for L1 composition (recall Table 18). As shown in Appendix F, her L1 composition had exactly the same content in the same order as in the notes, including more repeats and paraphrases from the notes than did her L2 composition. In contrast, in her notes for L2 composition, she made a list of her thoughts or ideas for both positions. Upon starting to write in L2, she reported that she had roughly planned what to write up to the end and that she was going to write referring to the notes. Consequently, she took more than 10 minutes longer to complete the L2 composition once she started to write. In L2, Ginko scored the least in the high group (recall Table 15). Her less detailed planning for L2 writing did not seem to help her produce a good writing product.

Chapter 4

L1 and L2 Writing Processes: Low versus High L2 Proficiency Level Students

Based on the results of the protocol analysis, in the preceding two chapters the two groups' L1 and L2 writing processes were compared within the respective groups. The results of intra-group comparison indicated that the lower-proficiency group showed differences in L1/L2 writing, but the higher-proficiency group did not differ much in terms of the type and frequency of strategies used. In this chapter, the L1/L2 writing processes are compared between the two groups respectively and the findings of comparing L1/L2 writing processes are summarized in the final section.[1]

Results and Discussion

L1 and L2 Writing Products

In general, the overall length of compositions is considered an index of students' writing fluency (Reid, 1990; Silva, 1993). The composition lengths provide important complementary information to writing process analysis. Process measures used in the present study such as total time, prewriting time, and the number of pauses and strategies should be considered in relation to the amount of text produced. In the present study, the total numbers of words/characters, sentences and paragraphs

Table 23: Mean Total Number of Characters/Words, Sentences, and Paragraphs

	Characters/Words M (SD) L1	Characters/Words M (SD) L2	Sentences M (SD) L1	Sentences M (SD) L2	Paragraphs M (SD) L1	Paragraphs M (SD) L2
Low	448.0 (114.9)	132.8 (48.1)	10.4 (4.4)	10.2 (4.0)	1.2 (0.45)	1.8 (0.84)
High	609.8 (128.1)	168.0 (39.3)	12.0 (1.7)	12.3 (1.6)	3.7 (0.2)	3.7 (0.6)

Table 24: Mean Number of Characters/Words Produced per Minute

	L1	L2
Low	20.43	4.35
High	22.12	6.14

per composition were counted to measure the text lengths (see Table 23). To measure writing fluency, the number of characters/words produced per minute was calculated for both groups. The total numbers of characters/words were divided by the writing time (i.e., total time spent minus time spent on prewriting). As Table 24 reveals, the high group produced slightly more characters/words, and thus showed more writing fluency in both L1 and L2 than the low group.

Regarding inter-language comparison, although it was impossible to compare the total number of words (L2) with that of characters (L1), it was possible to compare the total number of sentences and paragraphs, respectively, between L1 and L2. As Table 23 shows, a similar tendency emerged in both measures. More specifically, each group produced almost the same number of L1/L2 sentences and paragraphs. Furthermore, the Mann-Whitney U tests were conducted to check for statistically significant differences between the two groups in the number of sentences and paragraphs of L1/L2 compositions. The results of the tests revealed that the differences between the groups were significant for the number of paragraphs in both L1 and L2: $z=-2.74$, $p=.006$; $z=-2.19$, $p=.0285$, respectively. The high proficiency group students were found to produce a significantly larger number of paragraphs in L1 and L2 than the low proficiency group students. This finding should also be taken as an indication that the high students were concerned with paragraphing, whereas the low students lacked such concern while writing. As sample L1/L2 compositions written by high and low group students exemplified (see Appendixes B, C, D, E, F, and G), only the former group of students paragraphed L1/L2 compositions properly.

L1 and L2 Writing Processes

(1) Prewriting Time and Total Writing Time

As Table 25 shows, the two groups did not differ much from each other in terms of time spent on prewriting. Both groups took slightly more time for prewriting in L2. In both L1 and L2, the high group used slightly more prewriting time than the low group. This finding accords with those of previous research (e.g., Bereiter & Scardamalia, 1987). As explained in Chapter 3, the high students did global planning (**Pp**) before starting to write in L1/L2. On the other hand, some low students only planned the opening sentence before writing. This difference in what they did before writing the first sentence may partly account for why the high students spent more prewriting time than did the low students in

Table 25: Mean Total and Prewriting Times

	Total Time Spent		Time Spent on Prewriting	
	L1	L2	L1	L2
Low	25:40	34:28	3:44	3:56
High	31:46	31:55	4:12	4:33

Note: 25:40 = minutes: seconds

both L1 and L2.

Regarding total time spent, there were more conspicuous differences between the two groups. As Table 25 shows, the high group did not differ much between L1 and L2 total writing time, whereas the low group spent more than 8 minutes longer in L2 writing. Because the two groups did not differ much in terms of prewriting time, this means that the low group consumed much more time once they started writing in L2. This finding is in accord with other studies that reported L2 writing took more time than L1 writing (Silva, 1993; Uzawa & Cumming, 1989). Contrastively, in L1, the low group needed 6 minutes less total writing time than the high group. The low group's confounding findings between L1 and L2 total time suggest that low students required much more time in L2 to produce similar length texts, in terms of the number of sentences and paragraphs, as in L1. Different from the low students, the high group produced L1/L2 texts of similar length, taking more or less the same amount of time. This finding implies that once L2 learners have reached a certain L2 proficiency/writing ability level, they needed no more writing time in L2 than in L1.

(2) Number of Pauses and Strategies

Table 26 presents means and *SD*s for numbers of pauses and strategies the two groups used. Both groups paused more frequently and employed substantially more strategies while writing in L2. However, the difference in the number of pauses in L1 and L2 was not found to be statistically significant: $z=-1.78$, $p=.075$, nor was the difference in the number of strategies: $z=-1.48$, $p=.139$ by the Wilcoxon Matched-Pairs Signed Ranks test. Only the pauses were found to be marginally more frequent in L2 ($p=.075$). Furthermore, the results of Mann-Whitney U tests revealed that the differences between the two L2 proficiency groups were not significant for either pauses or strategies in L1 and L2.

Nevertheless, as Table 26 shows, the low group paused more than the high group in both L1 and L2. Because writing without pausing can be considered contributory to fluent writing (Sasaki & Hirose, 1996), the finding that the high students paused less than the low students to produce lengthier compositions implied that the former wrote more fluently than the latter group. As for strategies, it is noteworthy that the high group used more, although not significantly, than the low group in both L1 and L2.

Table 26: Mean Number of Pauses and Strategies

	Pauses M(SD) L1	L2	Strategies M(SD) L1	L2
Low	16.4 (5.1)	22.0 (12.2)	21.4 (6.7)	29.0 (12.7)
High	14.2 (3.9)	19.5 (2.5)	29.5 (8.9)	34.2 (9.0)

(3) Quantitative Analysis of Strategies

Table 27 lists the mean number of strategies used by the two groups. It shows that both groups of students employed similar writing strategies, whereas each group also resorted to writing strategies not so frequently used by the other group, in both L1 and L2 writing. Table 27

Table 27: Mean Number of Strategies Used

	Planning P_P P_L P_O P_C	Retrieval R_P R	Generation G A	Verbalization T L L_L L_C F	Re-reading E	Others
L1 Low	0.4 4.2 0.4 1.0	0.4 0.2	1.0 0.8	1.6 0.4 3.4 0 0	7.2	0.4
High	1.0 1.8 0.7 1.5	1.0 1.2	0.5 0.8	3.3 3.0 2.7 1.0 0.7	10.2	0.2
L2 Low	0.4 5.2 0 1.2	1.6 0.4	0.4 1.2	8.4 1.0 5.0 0 0	4.2	0
High	1.0 1.3 0.8 1.7	1.3 0.2	0.3 1.0	5.3 5.0 4.3 0.8 0.2	8.7	2.2

reveals that reader consciousness (L_C) and knowledge about composition (F) were used only by high students.

Table 28 presents the five (or six) most frequently used strategies. Of these strategies, four strategies were exactly the same in L1/L2 between the two groups (L_L, E, P_L, and T), whereas the remaining one or two were different. The common strategy use between the two groups shows that they paused mostly to verbalize prepositions, reread what had been written, plan locally and correct the surface forms both in L1 and L2. The results also implied that strategies cross languages. Those strategies not employed in L1 did not have a place in L2 either. The differences in strategy use between the two groups reveal that there was a strategy each group used that was not so frequently used by the other group. More specifically, it was characteristic of the high group to use global planning (P_p) and refining rhetoric (L) in both L1 and L2. On the other hand, although the high group also used P_L, it was more characteristic of the low group to use P_L (local planning) in both L1 and L2.

Table 28: The Five Highest Ratios of Strategies Used according to Group

	Low		High	
L1	E (Rereading)	33.6%	E (Rereading)	34.6%
	P_L (Local Planning)	19.6%	T (Verbalizing Propositions)	11.2%
	L_L (Correcting Surface Forms)	15.9%	L (Refining Rhetoric)	10.2%
	T (Verbalizing Propositions)	7.5%	L_L (Correcting Surface Forms)	9.2%
	P_C (Conclusion Planning)	4.7%	P_L (Local Planning)	6.1%
	G (Spontaneous Idea Generation)	4.7%		
L2	T (Verbalizing Propositions)	29.0%	E (Rereading)	25.4%
	P_L (Local Planning)	17.9%	T (Verbalizing Propositions)	15.5%
	L_L (Correcting Surface Forms)	17.2%	L (Refining Rhetoric)	14.6%
	E (Rereading)	14.5%	L_L (Correcting Surface Forms)	12.5%
	R_p (Retrieving Plans)	5.5%	P_L (Local Planning)	3.8%
			R_p (Retrieving Plans)	3.8%

Furthermore, it is interesting that each group shows a pattern different from the other in the order of the most frequently used strategies. The high group used the same five strategies in exactly the same order of frequency in L1/L2. In contrast, the low group had a different order of most frequently used strategies. In L2, the ratio of rereading (**E**) occupied 14.5%, as opposed to 33.6% in L1. Conversely, in L2, the ratio of verbalizing propositions (**T**) constituted almost 30% of all the strategies used, as opposed to less than 10% in L1. In the case of the high students, the ratios of **T** in L1/L2 did not differ much. These findings implied that low students encountered much more difficulty verbalizing their intended meaning in L2, whereas high students did not.

(4) Qualitative Analysis of Strategies
1) Comparisons of L1 Writing Processes between the Two Groups

As explained above, L1 writing processes of the two groups had both similarities and differences. Both groups paused to reread (**E**) most frequently (Table 28), but for different reasons. The low group mostly reread either to plan what to write next (**P$_L$**) or to correct/think of surface forms like Chinese characters (**L$_L$**). On the other hand, the high group tended to reread not only for verbalizing thoughts into language (**T**) but also for seeking more refined expressions (**L**). In L1, the high-proficiency students paused more for verbalization-related purposes such as **T** and **L**, than low students. As an example of **T**, Ichiro pondered after writing "自宅にて、" (=at home) in the second paragraph (see Appendix B). He reported that, although the ideas were present, he took time thinking of how effectively to verbalize them. As an example of **L**, Hikari first wrote "以前から" (=since before) in the first sentence, erased it, and wrote "明治以降" (=since the Meiji Era) instead because she considered the previous expression ambiguous (see Appendix C). Moreover, the high-proficiency students were concerned with appropriateness of expressions not only from the writer's but also from the readers' points of view. Ichiro, for example, wrote how Americans celebrate Christmas, and then he wondered whether he should add a Canadian example to it because things were basically the same in Canada and the U.S.. He decided to include Canadian information because the letter to the editor in the newspaper is presupposed to be read by various readers, who would require concrete examples. Thus, his awareness of the readers (L_C) led him to add his Canadian experience at Christmas time (see Appendix B).

Thus, it has been shown that the two groups of students monitored and evaluated what was being written down while writing, but in different ways. The low-proficiency students were mainly concerned about the surface forms. Furthermore, they paused more to do local planning than the high-proficiency students (recall Table 28).

The two groups of students also differed even when they employed global planning (P_P). As has been discussed, P_P was more characteristic of the high group because all high students did global planning in L1/L2 (recall Table 20). On the other hand, only 2 low students did global planning in L1/L2 (recall Table 13). Despite using P_P, furthermore, these students failed to produce as high-level L1/L2 compositions as high-proficiency students did. This finding raises questions about the effects of employing good writers' strategies because the finding implies that simply using good writers' strategies did not necessarily result in producing good compositions (see Chapter 6 for similar observations).

Similarly, the two groups of students appeared to approach conclusion planning (P_C) differently. For example, 2 low students only somewhat planned their conclusions, or, more exactly, they decided to simply finish with the sentence being constructed probably because they felt their ideas running out. The other 3 low students clearly planned how to finish because they attempted to make a good final remark in the final sentence. They all expressed difficulty ending with a good closing. Although such difficulty was shared by some high students, the high students planned to end more specifically with a paragraph or sentence that included a summary or conclusion.

2) Comparisons of L2 Writing Processes between the Two Groups

As in the case of L1 writing processes, the two groups of students employed similar strategies, but not necessarily in the same ways while writing in L2. As in L1 writing processes, it was characteristic of the low students to use P_L and L_L, and of the high students to employ P_P and **L**. Furthermore, high students had concerns over whether the readers would understand the intended meaning or not (L_C). The high students' frequent use of **L** is consistent with the finding of Sasaki (2000), who found the "expert" writers, unlike "novice" writers, used this strategy most frequently in L2. Similarly, Cumming's (1989) professionally experienced writers were found to take time choosing the most appropriate word and monitoring it in terms of meaning and appropriateness.

I limit my discussion in this section to the use of **T**, because both groups of students employed them frequently (recall Table 28) but somewhat differently.

As discussed in Chapter 2, in terms of verbalizing propositions (**T**), low students experienced more difficulty translating their intended meaning into L2. They tended to plan what to write in L1, and then they attempted to replace L1 with L2 rigidly. They searched for the equivalent L2 expressions of L1, only to fail to find one and instead modify or sometimes distort their intended meaning using the limited expressions they had access to. For example, Beni reported having stumbled over translating such expressions as "朝の少ない時間" (= limited time in the morning), "おしゃれしている" (= making himself fashionable) and "反抗期" (=

the period of rebelliousness) in her L1 notes (see Appendix G). Her clause "he enjoys wearing his school cloths" was intended to mean that he fully enjoys considering himself to look fashionable even under the constraints of wearing a school uniform. As for "反抗期" she gave up searching for the L2 equivalent word and used an L1 verb "反抗する" (= rebel) preceding "their parents," thus producing a paraphrase consisting of both L1 and L2 words.

By contrast, high-proficiency students did not report having translation problems explicitly as low students did. They were more likely to write directly in L2 and to make vocabulary or syntactical choices consciously when they were faced with the choice or assessment. At word level, for example, Fumi debated which verb ("keep" or "obey") ought to precede "our rules," and chose "keep" as in the following clause: "we have to keep our rules." At word level, but also including stylistic concerns, Hikari faced a word choice between "atmosphere" and "environment," to produce the following clause: "School should offer an ideal atmosphere for students to study hard"(see Appendix C). She assessed that the word "atmosphere" was more appropriate to express her intended meaning. Furthermore, they also encountered syntactic and semantic level choices. For example, Fumi paused over how to express that students have to follow school rules. What she ended up with was: "Students have to wear their uniforms as far as their rules say they have to wear them." High-proficiency students searched for the right word or syntactic structure that was not only linguistically correct but also appropriate in the sense that it fit their intended meaning, assessed the alternatives retrieved, and subsequently made a choice.

These contrasting results concerning the role of L1 in L2 writing imply that reliance on L1, or L1/L2 switching in L2 writing, may be a distinguishing factor between the two groups. The low-proficiency group's preoccupation with lexical replacement from L1 to L2 versus the high-proficiency group's concern over a better match between intention and expression is in accordance with the finding of de Larios, Murphy, and Manchon (1999). They found advanced Spanish students of English had recourse to ideational and textual reformulations, whereas intermediate students turned to compensating for linguistic deficiencies.

In connection to the role of L1 use in L2 writing, the use of notes should be taken into consideration. Both groups of students, 3 low-proficiency and 3 high-proficiency students wrote notes before beginning to write. Those students used L1 except for an occasional word or a phrase in L2. Unlike high students who made notes for global planning mostly before beginning to write, low students who made notes resorted to local planning in L1 while writing. For example, while writing in L2, Emi wrote a sentence in L1, revised the Japanese sentence in light of L2 vocabulary she could manage to activate, and then translated it into an L2 sentence. This successive process of switching between writing in L1 and transposing to L2 facilitated her L2 writing production. On the other hand, Beni started to write the first sentence when her plan of what to write was complete except the final part. Unlike Emi, she first wrote down her global plan (see Appendix G). Compared with her notes for L1 writing, those for L2 writing were more integrated into her L2 composition. She mostly translated the L1 notes into L2 in the same order. In fact, she added only two more sentences to the translated version of her notes, namely a sentence following "in short time I wore it" and the final sentence. Although Beni and Emi differed in their planning, both made use of L1 to generate content and both clung to their L1 notes to produce L2 compositions. It is not a coincidence that Beni and Emi were the most frequent users of **T** in the group (recall Table 13). Thus, for low students, too, making plans in L1 and then translating them into L2 may be a compensatory strategy to overcome their highly limited L2 proficiency level/writing ability.

In contrast, high-proficiency students did not seem to engage in direct translation from L1 to L2 even when they wrote down notes in L1. Their use of L1 in L2 writing was more complex and difficult to detect. Just as Beni did, Ginko prepared notes, which were referred to while writing (see Appendix F). On the other hand, unlike Emi, Ginko did not resort to direct translation. For example, with reference to "動きにくい" (= difficult to move) in her notes, she reported having wondered how to express it in L2. She ended up integrating the following into the previous main clause: "uncomfortable especially around the neck." There are gaps between the literal translation "difficult to move" and the final expression. In fact, the latter had a more specific meaning. This implied that Ginko did not translate L1 pretexts into L2 texts as Beni did. Ginko's L2 composition did not reflect her notes as much as Beni's L2 composition did (compare their L2 compositions in Appendixes F and G). Fumi also prepared notes, which had her position and reasons, before writing the first sentence. While writing, she circled some sentences or added some new sentences to the notes, thus she used her notes for local planning, too. Cumming (1989) pointed to two types of planning found in expert writers, which are advance planning and emergent planning. Fumi exemplified these two types of planning using notes in her L2 writing. She used her notes to generate content and plan. While writing, she also made decisions on what to write from the notes.

Given the limited time in which to write, it was faster for them to plan in their L1. For some high students in the present study, it may be regarded as a compensatory strategy to make up for their still limited L2 proficiency level/writing ability. Thus, there is a possibility that L1 use at the planning stage can activate L2 writing even for advanced L2 students.

The use of L1 at the planning stage is a controversial issue, that is, whether using L1 in planning facilitates or hinders actual L2 writing. Nevertheless, as discussed above, high and low students apparently used L1 notes differently from each other in writing. The results of the present study showed that the functions of planning in the form of L1 notes are used differently in writing process according to the student's proficiency level. Furthermore, the results implied that the effects of using L1 pretexts on L2 writing quality vary with the level. It was the low-proficiency students who used L1 notes that benefited from using them. Those students who relied on the L1 notes, Emi and Beni, scored the best and the second best, respectively, in the low group (recall Table 8). Contrastively, Ginko and Fumi, the most extensive note-takers in the high group, scored the least and the second least in the group (recall Table 15). The other note-taker, Ichiro, only wrote down a brief outline in his notes, and the remaining 3 high students did not use notes at all. For high students, therefore, the effects of the L1 notes on L2 writing product seemed to be less evident. This finding does not concur with Zamel (1983), who reported the student who planned in L1 produced the best L2 composition among the advanced-level ESL students. Regarding the effects of L1 use on L2 writing, Kobayashi and Rinnert (1992) found they varied with their L2 proficiency level. In their study, the lower proficiency level Japanese EFL students produced significantly better L2 compositions by translating from their previously composed L1 compositions than those written by direct writing in L2, whereas higher-proficiency students did not show such differences between their two L2 compositions written in such different ways.[2] The findings of the present analysis seem to be consistent with their findings. They imply that L1 use and translation can be employed as an aid to facilitate L2 production for inexperienced L2 writers.

As the protocol analysis in Chapters 2 and 3 revealed, it is difficult to rule out the use of L1 or translation even when they did not write down any notes in L1. As discussed in Chapter 2, low-proficiency students had a tendency to rely on translation. For example, Aya deliberately switched from translating her planned L1 sentences to direct writing in L2. Although she did not write notes in L1 from that time on, it was highly probable that she made L1-L2 translations at a word or phrase level mentally. On the other hand, high-proficiency students resorted to L1 differently. Jiro, who did not prepare notes, reflected that while writing in L2, he got stuck with several words that stayed in L1 in his mind, and he paused to make an appropriate word choice in such cases. Specifically, he pointed to two L1 words, "用意" (= preparation) and "家計" (= family budget) that preoccupied him most. He ended up with the following sentence: "When uniforms are not adopted, the students should therefore have a lot of (and almost excessive) clothings, which would be some burden to their family (income) in the long run." In the sentence, "用意" was turned into "have" and "家計" into "their family (income)."

It is no doubt that knowledge about the topic (= school uniforms) was retrieved from memory in L1 in the present study. This topical knowledge in L1 might have exerted inescapable influences on their dominant use of L1 in planning what to write both globally and locally. The role and the use of L1 in L2 writing should be considered in relation to a topic. Topics related to the writers' experience in L1 were found to facilitate more L1 use (see Krapels, 1990, for a review). Furthermore, Friedlander (1990) gave evidence that using L1 to generate content actually led to better planning and better writing products.

Thus, the findings of Part II suggest that both nature and extent of L1 use in L2 writing vary with the writer's L2 proficiency level, and the amount of L1 use decreases as the writer's L2 proficiency develops.

Wang and Wen (2002) investigated Chinese EFL students' amount of L1 use in L2 writing based on their think-aloud data and found the amount of L1 use decreased with the development of the students' L2 proficiency level. They calculated the numbers of Chinese (L1) and English (L2) words divided by the total number of words in the protocol. For argumentative writing, on average, the students used L1 in the proportion of 24% of the think-aloud protocol data. On the other hand, Cumming (1990) claimed no such relation between writing expertise level and L1 use. In order to resolve this inconclusive issue, we need more quantitative studies that deal with amount of L1 in L2 writing. Equally importantly, much more in-depth qualitative studies that focus on the nature of L1 use in L2 writing should also follow up. The role of L1 in L2 writing should be further elucidated in future studies.

The recall protocol data I collected in L1 after the participants finished L2 writing provided rich information to analyze their writing processes. However, the data were limited as resources to vigorously examine the amount and functions of their L1 use during L2 writing. For this purpose, a better method to capture L1 use during L2 writing should be devised. The concurrent method can be a candidate, but think-aloud data are also limited in that they do not include the information of what the writers are doing during pauses unless they express their thoughts in the spoken language either in L1 or L2. Furthermore, in whichever language they think aloud, this will inevitably affect their L2 writing process.

Summary of Part II

By using recall protocols to compare the L1 and L2 writing processes of each individual student, Part II of the present volume found both similarities and differences between the two processes within an individual writer. Product analysis supplemented process analysis, and the qualitative analysis of the protocols provided important information that was not captured by the quantitative analysis alone.

The following is a summary of the findings in Chapter 2.

1. The L1/L2 compositions written by low proficiency Japanese EFL students were of similar length in terms of the numbers of sentences and paragraphs. The students wrote slightly more than a paragraph in L1/L2 and did not indent properly in either language.
2. The students' L1 and L2 writing processes differed in terms of total writing time, but the processes did not differ in terms of prewriting time, or the numbers of strategies and pauses used while writing. Furthermore, there were individual differences in L2 writing processes.
3. The differences between L1 and L2 writing processes lay mostly in the "verbalization" stage (T). In L2, lower-proficiency students paused to do lexical retrieval or search while accommodating their present proficiency levels. A higher frequency of **T** in L2 appears to show that the students had problems translating their ideas into L2 after they formed them in L1. Their word search often resulted in failure, because wrong or non-existent L2 words were selected.
4. In both L1 and L2, the students were concerned with correct surface forms (spelling and grammar). This finding does not seem to concur with unskilled writers' characteristics reported in previous studies (e.g., Raimes, 1985). On the other hand, the students did not show concern for the reader, appropriateness of expressions, or paragraphing. Thus, they did not use good writers' strategies reported in previous studies (e.g., Cohen,

1990).

5. In both L1 and L2, the students tended to rely on local planning (**P$_L$**), but some actually employed global planning (**Pp**). However, those who used **Pp** did not organize better than those students unconcerned with global planning.

6. Thus, for lower L2 proficiency level students, limited L2 proficiency did not appear to be the only hindering factor for L2 writing. Their common use of **P$_L$**, and non-use of **L**, **L$_C$** and F in L1/L2 writing implied that they were also prevented from developing efficient L1 writing skills and/or had acquired insufficient knowledge of writing. Furthermore, even the employment of a good writers' strategy (**Pp**) did not result in good writing products.

Subsequently, Chapter 3 revealed how advanced Japanese EFL students' L2 writing was related to and different from their L1 writing. Based on the results of analyses of writing processes and products, the following summary can be made concerning the high-proficiency students' L1 and L2 writing.

1. The quantity of L1/L2 compositions written by advanced Japanese EFL students did not differ much in terms of the numbers of sentences and paragraphs.

2. Their protocols as well as their compositions revealed that the students had a sense of paragraphing in L1 and L2.

3. Their L1 and L2 writing processes did not differ much in terms of the total time spent, time spent on prewriting, and numbers and ratios of strategies used while writing. This finding is similar to that of Arndt (1987), who found L1/L2 writing of advanced-level EFL Chinese students were generally similar.

4. In both L1 and L2, the students were concerned with not only linguistic (lexical and syntactic) choices but also appropriateness of expressions, coherence and the reader. These features matched good writers' characteristics depicted in past research (e.g., Cohen, 1990). On the other hand, they did not accord with the findings of previous studies on inexpert

or novice Japanese EFL writers (e.g., Uzawa, 1996).
5. The results of the qualitative analysis indicated that they actually differed in their global planning and in their lexical/syntactical selection processes between L1 and L2. More specifically, lexical or syntactical choices sometimes required the students to make more conscious, time-consuming engagements in L2.
6. With linguistic advantages in L1 writing, their L1 writing process was more spontaneous. This spontaneous nature of L1 writing process caused some students difficulty in organizing their arguments but at the same time probably induced more varied organizations as shown in Chapter 1.

Finally, the following findings are enumerated based on the comparisons made in Chapter 4.
1. The findings that high proficiency level students' L1/L2 writing process had many similarities and those of low students did not in terms of the measures used in the present study suggest that L2 writing process becomes more similar to L1 writing process as their L2 proficiency develops.
2. Both high and low proficiency level students' planning strategies were similar in L1 and in L2 writing. This finding corresponds to the findings of previous studies (e.g., Jones & Tetroe, 1987; McDonough, 1995). The present study suggests that L1 writing strategies, particularly planning strategies, are transferable to L2 writing.
3. The two groups' L1 writing processes were different in terms of planning and verbalization. The lower-proficiency students paused more to plan, and the higher-proficiency students paused more to verbalize their intended meaning.
4. The difference between the two proficiency groups in L2 writing was found to lie in the verbalization process. The lower-proficiency group tended to resort to L1-L2 translation at word or phrase level, whereas the higher group attempted to match their intended meaning with the appropriate expressions.
5. Process analysis of the present study revealed Japanese EFL writers

were of great variety in terms of use of writing strategies. This finding is similar to those in previous studies (Arndt, 1987; Raimes, 1985).

Part III

Examining the Effects of L2 Writing Instruction on Student Writing

Chapter 5
Instruction on English Paragraph Organization

In Part III, I focus on English writing courses Japanese university students take for the first time formally. These courses can be considered important for several reasons in the Japanese context. First of all, this type of course is usually one of the students' first exposures to English writing instruction. As discussed in Part I, Japanese students have not had much experience writing English nor received formal English writing instruction prior to university entrance. Thus, we should devise such English writing courses that include content and methods these students need. In these courses, we should target especially those students who are like the low group students in Parts I and II of the present volume. As revealed in Part II, no low students paused to use knowledge about composition. This may imply they lack knowledge about L2 writing conventions such as indentation. What knowledge about L2 writing these students lack should be investigated to design an L2 writing course for them. Different from the high students, the low students did not properly indent or form a paragraph (see Appendixes D, E, and G). This was one of the differences found between the two groups' English writings.

Considering the limitations of the sentence-level translation practice on students' L2 writing ability, English teachers in Japan have given attention to paragraph-level English writing instruction for quite some time now (Hashiuchi, 1995). Such writing instruction includes a variety of teaching, ranging from teaching about English paragraphs (e.g., topic sentence, coherence, and organizational patterns such as cause and effect) to providing students with writing experiences (e.g., structured paragraph writing or free journal writing). This chapter is confined to teaching knowledge about English paragraphs and examines the effects of teaching on students' subsequent English writing.[1] Chapter 6 investigates the effects of journal writing experience and writing strategy instruction. Taking these two types of writing instruction into account serves the purpose of exploring the teaching effects to pursue the possibility of implementing them in the classroom.

English Paragraph Writing Instruction

The English writing instruction reported in this chapter consists of explicitly teaching paragraph elements such as the topic sentence, the body, and concluding sentence, and the types of organizational patterns (description, presentation of one's opinion and supporting it, etc.). Such instruction fits well with the "current-traditional rhetoric approach," combining the "current-traditional paradigm" from L1 English composition instruction with contrastive rhetoric (Silva, 1990). Although the "current-traditional rhetoric approach" has been criticized for its strong focus on form, discouraging creative aspects of writing (Silva, 1990), it can be helpful to those Japanese students who do not have much knowledge about English paragraph structure.

The present empirical study was motivated by the following four concerns. First, as revealed in Parts I and II of the present volume, the weak writers did not know much about English paragraphs. For example, they did not even know what a paragraph looked like. They lacked knowledge beyond a sentence level in English. In fact, such knowledge about English paragraphs was one of the significant factors that influenced the quality of Japanese students' English writing (Sasaki & Hirose, 1996), and teaching it explicitly can be expected to improve students' L2 writing ability. Second, although such instruction of paragraph-level writing has been actually in practice, empirical research has not been done sufficiently regarding its effects. Furthermore, previous studies have found mixed results concerning the teaching effects on Japanese students' L2 English writing. On one hand, positive effects have been reported. For example, Fukushima (1985) compared the compositions students wrote before and after such an English composition course, and described some improvements found in the post-compositions (e.g., paragraphing or coherence). On the other hand, some studies suggest that students, given English paragraph writing instruction, do not necessarily transfer the learned knowledge directly to their actual writing. For example, Hirose and Sasaki (2000) found that although students gained the knowledge after the instruction, they did not improve their writing in any major way except mechanics. Third, a controversy over the effects of English paragraph writing can be partly derived from the participants' L2 writing ability levels which could cover a wide range of students like both the high and low students in Parts I and II of the present volume. Reporting on the effects of teaching English transition words on Japanese college students' writing, Fukushima and Sato (1989) implied that the effects might vary according to the students' initial writing ability. Therefore, it can be speculated that the effects of L2 writing instruction would differ relative to students' L2 writing ability. Last, previous longitudinal studies that investigated the instructional effects on student subsequent writing have taken the teachers' (= raters') evaluation as the sole data (e.g., Hirose & Sasaki, 2000). Unlike these studies, the present chapter included the students' self-evaluation comparing compositions written before and after an instruction in its investigation. This is because it can also give insight into if and why (or why not) improvements are made after the instruction.

Research Questions

Thus, the present chapter addresses the following three research questions:

1. Does the teaching of English paragraph writing have an effect on Japanese students' L2 writing?
2. Do teaching effects differ dependent on students' L2 writing ability?
3. How do Japanese students evaluate the effects themselves?

Method

Participants

A total of 22 Japanese university students (10 men and 12 women) taking a course titled "English Composition I" at a public university night school participated in the present segment of the study.[2] This was the first English composition course they took at the university. Participant English proficiency, based on the CELT Form A, varied from low-intermediate to advanced (see Table 29).

For *Research Question 2*, I chose 7 good writers (1 men and 6 women) and 7 weak writers (6 men and 1 women) from the 22 participants. The selection was made based on the compositions they wrote before the instruction: good writers had scored more than 160 out of 200 (80%), whereas weak scored less than 125 (62.5%). The two writer groups of the present chapter roughly corresponded to those of the high and low L2 proficiency groups in Parts I and II of the present volume. The high and low groups in the previous parts had mean scores of 158.8 and 105.8 for English composition, respectively (recall Table 6).

According to Jacobs et al. (1981), the good writer group in the present chapter can be categorized into "very good to excellent" L2 writers,[3] whereas the weak writer group falls approximately into "poor to fair." Regarding the two groups' English proficiency levels, the mean CELT score for good writers was 225.1 (Range: 187-264), and that for weak writers was 148.3 (Range: 121-186).

Table 29: Descriptive Statistics of Participants' CELT Scores ($N=22$)

Measure (total possible)	M	SD	Range
CELT Listening (100)	60.8	15.3	40 - 96
CELT Structure (100)	67.8	15.4	36 - 91
CELT Vocabulary (100)	51.8	17.0	32 - 93
CELT Total (300)	180.4	44.0	121 - 264

Content of Instruction on English Paragraphs

All participants received instruction on English paragraphs in an English composition course. The course met once a week for 90 minutes for a 12-week semester. Based on a coursebook (Kitao & Kitao, 1988), the instruction consisted of teaching the knowledge of an English paragraph by means of reading and analyzing sample paragraphs. The coursebook was written entirely in English. The teaching content included the following (see Chapter 1 through Chapter 6 in Kitao & Kitao, 1988, for details):[4]

What is a paragraph?

The parts of a paragraph (introduction, discussion, conclusion)

Topic sentence

Characteristics of a good paragraph (unity, coherence, use of transition words)

Descriptive paragraphs

Narrative paragraphs

Personal opinions

In each chapter, the book first explains an idea related to a paragraph with a model paragraph, and then provides exercises analyzing other paragraphs. In addition, a paragraph-level writing exercise is provided at the end of each chapter. These paragraphs (six in all) were completed as assignments.

Data

(1) Pre- and Post-Instruction Compositions

The participants wrote an argumentative composition entitled "Should women work after they get married?" before and after the instruction. In other words, they wrote on the same topic at the beginning and the end of the semester-long course. They wrote the post-compositions four months later as part of a final test for the course. On both occasions, the participants were not informed beforehand that they would be writing on the topic, and they were not allowed to use a dictionary. The same time limit (= 20 minutes) was set for both the pre- and post-compositions. Although this time limit was relatively short (Krapels, 1990), it was considered appropriate for students to write a paragraph-level composition. Further extension of the time limit was not possible because of the course schedule. I also took the following point made by Hale (1992) into consideration: "Livingston (1987) found that high school and college students given 30 minutes to write an essay did not score significantly higher than those given 20 minutes" (p. 3).

Both compositions were scored by two English L2 writing specialists, according to Jacobs et al.'s (1981) ESL Composition Profile. Ratings were judged according to five criteria: content, organization, vocabulary, language use, and mechanics. Each participant's score was the sum of the two raters' scores, with a possible range of 68 to 200 points. The total number of words per composition was also counted as a measurement of students' writing fluency (Reid, 1990).

(2) Students' Comparison of Pre- and Post-Instruction Compositions

The present analysis included the students' self-evaluations comparing their pre- and post-compositions. One month after they wrote the post-compositions, each of them was asked to read and analyze the pre- and post-compositions s/he wrote concerning the following three points: (a) whether the post-compositions improved in terms of the presentation of topic sentence and its supporting evidence; (b) whether they found differences between the two compositions; and (c) whether the instruction on topic sentence, unity, or coherence actually helped them to write post-compositions (if so, in what ways). Before they analyzed their own compositions, they learned such metalanguage as topic sentence, unity and coherence. When they compared the pre- and post-compositions, the students did not know their post-composition scores yet.[5] They gave open-ended responses to these points in written Japanese. All the quotes from written student analysis in this chapter were translated into English by me.

Data Analysis

For *Research Question 1*, the pre- and post-compositions of all participating students were compared in terms of the five subscores, total scores, and total number of words using paired *t*-tests. Because I made 6 comparisons in all for L2 composition scores, I divided the alpha level of 0.05 by the number of comparisons (i.e., 0.05/6), and accepted only those *t*-tests that were below the 0.0083 level as significant. For *Research Question 2*, good and weak writers' pre- and post-compositions were compared between the two groups, respectively, using the Mann-Whitney U test, a nonparametric test for comparisons between two groups. Because 6 comparisons were made, the alpha level of 0.05 was adjusted to 0.0083 by a Bonferroni correction. For *Research Question 3*, self-report data (from all participants' comparisons between pre- and post-compositions) were compiled based on analysis of their open-ended responses. In addition, good and weak writers' responses were compared where relevant.

Results and Discussion

Research Question 1: Comparisons of Pre- and Post-Instruction Compositions

Table 30 displays descriptive statistics for the total scores, the five subscores, and the total words of the pre- and post-compositions. Reliability estimates for the composition scores are interrater reliability estimates based on Pearson correlation coefficients. As shown in Table 30, reliability estimates for the composition scores were generally high except for the post-composition organization (0.54) and mechanics (0.32).

The latter was low probably because the full score for mechanics was as small as 10, and the *SD* was small (0.96). Thus, the results concerning these two subscores should be treated with caution. Regarding length, the post-compositions were shorter than the pre-compositions by 25.36 words (i.e., 19.3% decrease) on average.

Results of paired *t*-tests for pre- and post-composition measures revealed that there were significant differences in vocabulary ($t=-3.37$, $df=21$, $p=.0029$), mechanics ($t=-4.54$, $p=0.0002$), and the total number of words ($t=4.15$, $p=.0004$). However, there were no significant differences found for content ($t=-2.05$, $p=.053$), language use ($t=-1.78$, $p=.089$), organization ($t=-1.57$, $p=.13$), or total scores ($t=-2.65$, $p=.015$). Post-compositions were found to be improved in terms of vocabulary and mechanics, and to be significantly shorter than the pre-compositions.

Table 30: Descriptive Statistics of Pre- and Post-Instruction Composition Scores (*N*=22)

Measure (total possible)	Pre-Instruction *M*	*SD*	Reliability	Post-Instruction *M*	*SD*	Reliability
Comp. Total (200)	142.23	22.71	0.96	151.18	17.77	0.89
Content (60)	44.87	6.78	0.93	47.46	5.78	0.81
Organization (40)	29.36	4.74	0.80	30.96	3.84	0.54
Vocabulary (40)	28.41	4.76	0.86	30.18	4.19	0.85
Language Use (50)	32.23	6.78	0.91	34.05	5.72	0.87
Mechanics (10)	7.36	1.29	0.66	8.55	0.96	0.32
Total No. of Words	131.18	37.66	—	105.82	32.48	—

Given the English paragraph instruction, although they did not significantly improve the overall quality, the students improved their writing in terms of vocabulary and mechanics. These findings partially confirm those of a previous longitudinal study (Hirose & Sasaki, 2000), where the students did not improve their writing except in mechanics after receiving similar knowledge about English writing instruction with journal writing experience. The mechanics of the students' writing, which is concerned with spelling, punctuation, capitalization, and paragraphing (Jacobs et al., 1981), again improved as a result of the instruction. Knowledge instruction on an English paragraph including reading paragraphs seems to help students actually to form a paragraph. As in the previous study, organization, defined to include "ideas clearly stated/supported," "logical sequencing," and "cohesiveness" (Jacobs et al., 1981), did not improve statistically. However, these contrastive findings are interesting because the instruction covered both mechanics and organization. With the instruction and limited amount of writing practice given, facility for mechanics was easier to get than that for organization. Obviously organization is related to more complex aspects of writing processes. Compared with mechanics, therefore, organization seems to develop more slowly. The non-significant result of organization is also discussed later in relation to what the students thought about their organizations themselves.

Because the students significantly improved the use of vocabulary (range, word/idiom choice and usage, register, etc.) after the instruction, the teaching of English paragraph writing was found to have some positive effects on students' writing in more ways than the previous study (Hirose & Sasaki, 2000). Considering the relatively short length of the instruction, the present study's results suggest this type of English paragraph instruction (explicit knowledge teaching with model paragraphs and some practice writing) is a promising method to teach English writing to Japanese students. Nevertheless, it is too early to be conclusive about the effects of this instruction. In addition to this composition course, the students were taking three other English courses (two reading and one conversation) concurrently. Thus, we cannot rule out the possibility that other practice led them to improve their writing, too. Furthermore, we would need a control group to test the effects of this type of L2 writing instruction.

Regarding the number of the total words as an index of writing fluency, the significantly reduced number for the post-compositions suggests that the students did not write them as fluently as the pre-compositions. This could be another effect of the instruction (see the <u>Research Question 3</u> section for discussion). Because the overall quality of the post-compositions was found to be slightly better, although not significantly, than that of the pre-compositions (recall Table 30), the shortened length did not seem to have a negative influence on the overall quality. One caution here is that common sense dictates that number of words may be a better index of spontaneity than of good writing.

Research Question 2: Comparisons of Pre- and Post-Instruction Compositions between the Two Writer Groups

Tables 31 and 32 show the means and *SD*s of the weak and good writers' pre- and post-compositions, respectively. The two groups revealed a different tendency in the pre- and post-composition scores. On

Table 31: Pre- and Post-Instruction Composition Scores for Weak Writers (*n*=7)

Measure (total possible)	Pre-Instruction *M*	Pre-Instruction *SD*	Post-Instruction *M*	Post-Instruction *SD*
Composition Total (200)	117.29	8.52	137.86	17.48
Content (60)	38.00	3.46	43.86	5.61
Organization (40)	24.14	3.08	29.00	4.62
Vocabulary (40)	24.00	1.53	27.00	2.65
Language Use (50)	24.43	2.64	29.71	4.96
Mechanics (10)	6.71	0.76	8.29	0.95
Total Number of Words	101.29	29.29	79.43	29.79

Table 32: Pre- and Post-Instruction Composition Scores for Good Writers (*n*=7)

Measure (total possible)	Pre-Instruction *M*	SD	Post-Instruction *M*	SD
Composition Total (200)	169.29	8.46	170.14	8.36
Content (60)	53.14	2.91	52.43	4.20
Organization (40)	33.71	2.43	34.14	3.02
Vocabulary (40)	34.43	2.15	35.14	2.12
Language Use (50)	39.29	4.27	39.43	4.12
Mechanics (10)	8.71	0.95	9.00	0.82
Total Number of Words	163.43	30.83	134.86	29.98

average, the weak writers gained 20 points for the post-compositions, whereas the good did not display much difference between the two compositions. Regarding the number of words produced, however, both groups showed a similar pattern; i.e., they wrote shorter post-compositions than the pre-compositions. The weak writers decreased 21.86 words (21.6%), and the good writers 28.57 words (17.5%).

Concerning the pre-composition scores, the results of Mann-Whitney U tests revealed that the differences between the two groups were significant for total score ($z=-3.13$, $p=0.0017$), content ($z=-3.13$, $p=0.0017$), organization ($z=-3.07$, $p=0.0022$), vocabulary ($z=-3.13$, $p=0.0017$), language use ($z=-3.13$, $p=0.0017$), and mechanics ($z=-2.87$, $p=0.0040$). Regarding post-composition scores, the Mann-Whitney U tests found different, mixed results. The differences between the two groups were significant for total score ($z=-3.07$, $p=0.0022$), vocabulary ($z=-3.07$, $p=0.0022$), and language use ($z=-2.68$, $p=0.0073$), whereas there were no significant differences for content ($z=-2.49$, $p=0.013$), organization ($z=-2.36$, $p=0.018$), and mechanics ($z=-1.41$, $p=0.160$). The pre-composition scores of the good writer group were significantly higher than those of the weak writer group in all the measures examined before the instruction began. However, half of the post-composition measures were not found significant between the two groups.

These results imply that the effects of teaching differed dependent on students' L2 writing ability. It seems that the weak writers, rather than the good writers, benefited from the instruction. Although the good writers still wrote longer and substantially better post-compositions than the weak writers, they did not show any significant improvement in comparison with their own pre-compositions.

Why were there such differences found between the two groups? The instruction probably had little effect on the good writers' writing in terms of the scores examined because they were "good to excellent" L2 writers before they received the instruction (see Table 32 for their pre-composition scores). With this advanced level achieved, it would not be so easy to further improve their writing in terms of any aspect examined. In contrast, the instruction revealed to be effective for the weak writers who most likely had not reached such a level yet. It is encouraging for teachers to find that these students improved their L2 writing after they took the paragraph-level writing instruction for a semester.

The two groups' post-compositions in contrast to their pre-compositions are discussed by taking one student's pre- and post-compositions from each group as representative examples. The examples chosen from each group were typical in the sense that a weak writer gained a much higher score for post-composition, whereas a good writer did not, but both writers shortened the length in post-compositions. Both students' pre- and post-composition scores were higher than the group means, respectively (see Tables 31 and 32).

The following compositions were written by one of the weak writers. His post-composition shows improvements in many ways. One of the most obvious improvements is mechanics. The pre-composition is not properly indented, whereas the post-composition, although unfinished, consists of one identifiable indented paragraph. Second, although the topic sentence (i.e., the writer's position statement on the given topic, "Should women work after they get married?") is placed at the beginning sentence in both compositions, it is grammatically formed, and thus more clearly stated in the post-composition regardless of a question mark misplaced at the end of the sentence.[6] Furthermore, only in the post-composition, the writer used such transition words as "first," "second," and "third" in enumerating reasons to support his position. These helped him to get much higher score in the post-composition. His post-composition total score was 155, as opposed to the pre-composition counterpart 125.

A weak writer's pre-instruction composition

I will agree my wife at her working after I married. Of course it is natural that women work after they get married. Because the idea that women must not work after they get marrige is old idea, women have more liberty time.

But when their child will be born, the wife and the husband have to discuss the child. They must cooparate to keep their child life.

They should do their house work together. The wife doesn't have to do it alone.

The wife who is impossible to work after she get married seems to be sad. Women should more go out from house. (105 words)

The same weak writer's post-instruction composition

I think women should work after they get married? First because it is not good that women stop her job if they want to go on it. In short women have the right that they can do anything they hope, too. Second because it's strange that women have to do housework only like Japanese trasition. Usually mothers take care of their babies, but it is possible that fathers do it. If parents are busy, they can employ a housemide. Third because it is not good that the wise women go out from workplace. So Japanese (95 words)

The next pre- and post-compositions were written by one of the good writers. One of the obvious differences between the two is in the position of topic sentence. It is placed in the very last sentence in the pre-composition, whereas it is stated in the first sentence in the post-composition. Her pre-composition exemplifies a new case of an inductive organizational pattern in light of the findings of Part I (i.e., no participants placed the main idea in the end or took an inductive pattern in English). In fact, several other good writers in this chapter employed an inductive organization in the post-compositions as well as pre-compositions (see the Research Question 3 section for placement of topic sentence). Furthermore, the pre-composition presents a sharp contrast to her post-composition, which has the main idea at the beginning and shows a deductive pattern. Her differing choices in L2 organization seems to support the point made in Part I that organizing text involves a writer's decision making at the time of writing (see the Students' Perceptions of Instructional Effects section for what the writer said about her organizations). Second, as in the case of the weak writer above, she made use of such transition words as "first," "second," and "third" in enumerating supporting reasons only in the post-composition. Third, the pre-composition consists of three paragraphs, whereas the post-composition has only one paragraph. In spite of the markedly reduced length (i.e., 44.4% decrease in word number), her post-composition may be better in terms of clarity and compactness. These conspicuous differences could have been partly attributed to the instructional effects. Despite these differences between the two compositions, it is also noticeable that her pre- and post-composition received similar scores, 175 and 176, respectively. This case seems to give support to the finding of

Part I concerning relations between organizational patterns and evaluation. More specifically, the choice of the deductive pattern did not directly relate to a higher evaluation of organization or overall quality. It also suggests that, unlike in the case of the weak writer above, the composition scores do not necessarily reflect instructional effects (see the *Research Question 3* section for what the students had to say about their pre- and post-compositions).

A good writer's pre-instruction composition

How many women have things to do every day for their long marriage life? Housekeeping, shopping and playing tennis can not satisfy them forever. I heard some of my married friends complain that they were bored of those activities. They told that they needed changes and wanted to learn something new.

Keep working requires you to learn new jobs. In addition, when you change the place to work, you have to get used to your new co-workers. You can have the field to make efforts only for yourself apart from your husband. Marriage is not a reason enough to abandan all the chance you get from the work.

Both husband and wife should share their duties and responsibility in order to keep good relationship. This is approved by the recent trend many couples have taken. So women never have to quit working for marriage. (144 words)

The same good writer's post-instruction composition

Women should work after they get married. Working has three main advantages for women. First, working gives them a easy way to keep in contact with society. Some wives join in social activity to belong to a group out of their families, but working meets their needs easyly. Second, working requires women to improve their skills. For example, they have to make efforts to catch up the newest computer technology. Third, women can be independent economically by earning by themselves. (80 words)

The weak and good writers' pre- and post-compositions showed similar changes between pre- and post-compositions. Stating the topic sentence at the beginning and using transition words were such common changes made across the groups. The effects of teaching transition words can be expected to work immediately on student subsequent writing. On the other hand, there was another common feature, non-change, between pre- and post-compositions. That is, neither of the two groups tended to make a summary statement in the end. Despite the instruction on the conclusion with the restatement of the opinion or summarization of the arguments (see Note 4 for details), only a very few participants actually made such concluding statements. This is compatible with the findings of Part I of the present volume in that fewer students finished with a position statement/restatement or summary statement in English. Unlike the use of transition words and placement of topic sentence in the beginning, making the conclusive statements in the end did not appear to have an immediate influence on student writing. I refer to these findings from a writer's point of view in the *Research Question 3* section.

In summary, as found in Part I of the present volume, there was not much difference between the weak and good writers' English compositions in terms of organizational patterns. The results of the present chapter suggest that deductive pattern (i.e., in this case, position-statement precedes supporting the position with reasons) may not be difficult for Japanese students, regardless of their L2 proficiency levels, to learn to use, and explicit instruction proved effective in this respect (see Hirose, 2003c).

In the next section, I look at how the students perceived the effects of the instruction to be. Self-report data from all the participants' comparisons between the pre- and post-compositions are first analyzed. In order to examine further why varying effects were found in this section depending on their initial L2 writing ability, I then look at how the two groups of writers compared their own pre- and post-compositions respectively.

Research Question 3: Students' Evaluations of Instructional Effects

(1) Students' Evaluations of Topic Sentence and Supporting Evidence

In this chapter, the topic sentence was considered a writer's position-stating sentence, and the participants were asked if they stated their positions in their pre- and post-compositions. When asked whether they wrote a topic sentence, or expressed their position explicitly, 17 participants (77.3%) answered that they did so in their post-compositions, whereas only 10 participants (45.5%) did so in the pre-compositions. In other words, 7 (31.8%) wrote a topic sentence only in post-compositions. Similarly, 16 participants (72.7%) claimed they provided supporting evidence for their positions in the post-compositions, whereas only half of them (8) reported they did so in the pre-compositions. Therefore, the instruction on providing a topic sentence and supporting their positions seems to have helped the participating students to actualize that in their own L2 writing.

As far as the weak writers are concerned specifically, 5 out of 7 students provided both topic sentence and supporting evidence in their post-compositions, whereas 3 wrote a topic sentence, and 2 supported their positions in the pre-compositions. For example, the following pair of compositions written by a weak writer illustrate a contrast in terms of the absence/presence of a topic sentence. The writer reported that his position was stated only in the post-composition in the form of a topic sentence, and also the three-part structure of introduction, discussion, and conclusion was formed in the post-composition.

A weak writer's pre-instruction composition

> Now, I have a idea that men and women of position were even. But I think that every men must work when they become adult. And, if she want to work, he should agree with her; they don't have some trouble in their family.
>
> Most of women have a trouble. It was made when women have their baby. This is reason why women loss their job. It is natural that they should talk about it each other. (77 words)

The same weak writer's post-instruction composition

> I recommend that women should work after they get married. Because if they finish take care of their baby or child, they are free from it. So It regret they do nothing during their life. In fact, sombody work to find their life, and sombody work to learn something. I think that she gets something is storng. Therefore I think that women should work after they get married. (68 words)

In contrast, 6 out of 7 good writers reported writing a topic sentence supported by evidence in both pre- and post-compositions. The one good writer who reported not writing a topic sentence in either composition claimed that he believed it was not necessary to present an explicit topic sentence, and his position should be clear from between sentences without one. In other words, the good writers' pre- and post-compositions did not differ much in terms of the presentation of topic sentence and supporting evidence. For example, the following pair of compositions written by a good writer show such similarity between pre- and post-compositions.

A good writer's pre-instruction composition

Should women work after they get married? It is a difficult question for both men and women. Probably, it is one of the most disscutionable questions for young couples, before getting married.

One of the biggest reasons for that is the high living cost. According to the reacent survey, about 1/2 of married women work in Japan. (It is incrouded part time jobs.) So some of them have to work in a poor condition to support their family. I think if they did not have any fainancial problem quite a lot of women would not have to work.

Besides the financial difficulties, some of them want to continue working for their own carrier or interests. Though the working condition for them is not so good I think it is still a good move for all of women.

This question is very personal so, it is up to each individuals. (149 words)

The same good writer's post-instruction composition

Should wome work after they get married? It is a difficult question for both men and women. I think there are mainly two reasons for women to work after their marriage.

Firstly, living expense is very high so that many women have to work in order to support their family. In this case usually they work as part time workers.

Secondly, some of the women woul like to work for their own carear. After working several years, their jobs getting more attractive for them. It is natural for them to keep their jobs after getting married. In this case they usually work on steady jobs.

To think about these reasons, there would be no reason for that women should not work after they get married. With their husbands' help, I think it is good thing for them. (137 words)

This writer's pre- and post-compositions present a contrastive case from another good writer's counterparts quoted in the *Research Question 2* section. Although this chapter does not compare organizational patterns of student pre- and post-compositions specifically, these two good writers' post-compositions revealed different effects of instruction on subsequent writing. It appears to have exerted more influences on the student who changed the position of topic sentence. Furthermore, the good writer of the compositions above wrote more or less the same number of words, as opposed to the previous one who reduced the number substantially in the post-composition. It is also noteworthy that, although she used transition words in her post-composition, the writer did not apparently use her learned knowledge of stating the position initially, thus producing basically the overall inductive organization in both compositions. This shows counter to the findings of Part I of the present volume, in which the majority of participants were found to employ an deductive pattern in L2. Those participants who chose an inductive pattern in the present chapter belonged to the good writer group. The writer stated in her comparisons that she expressed her position in both, but she did so more explicitly in her post-composition. She expressed concerns over the post-topic sentence by acknowledging that the impact of the sentence was weak. The writer is right in that the topic sentence was more overtly stated, but still not so strongly, in the post-composition.

(2) Students' Perceived Differences between the Pre- and Post-Instruction Compositions

Reading and comparing their own pre- and post-compositions, all students except one (95.5%) pointed out there were differences between the two compositions. Two students (9.1%) found that their positions on the topic were completely opposite, and another two (9.1%) found their argumentation drastically different between the two compositions. Because they wrote the post-compositions four months after the pre-compositions, these changes may come as no surprise. Nevertheless, the majority (81.8%) of the participants stated the post-compositions were better than the pre-compositions in various ways, for example, use of transition words, persuasiveness, coherence, or easiness for readers to follow.

The good and weak writers both shared this positive view of the post-compositions. Their self-evaluations were mostly supported by higher scores on post-compositions, especially those written by weak writers. Unlike in the case of the weak writers, the good writers' post-compositions in terms of scores did not sufficiently reflect their positive evaluations. Why they evaluated them better than the weak writers did is discussed in the next section.

(3) Students' Perceptions of Instructional Effects

In response to the question inquiring whether the instruction helped them to actually write the post-compositions, 16 (72.7 %) of the participants reported that they attempted to use the learned knowledge of English paragraph organization while writing the post-compositions. For example, 7 participants (31.8%) contended that they paid attention to the overall organization; more specifically, they tried to organize the compositions with the three parts (i.e., introduction, discussion and conclusion), as the coursebook instructed them to do. In addition, 4 participants (18.2%) reported that they attempted to use transition words while writing post-compositions. The testing condition under which they wrote the post-compositions may have partly facilitated their conscious use of the learned knowledge. Despite their attention to the learned knowledge, however, many (40.9%) of the participants claimed that their post-compositions did not fulfill their attempts to a satisfactory level. Upon reading post-compositions a month later, students reported that these compositions showed less improvement in terms of the learned knowledge than they had expected. This reservation may require some discussion.

Trying to put the learned knowledge into practice, the students may have written the post-compositions differently from the pre-compositions. For example, one student explicitly stated that she wrote the pre-composition as she liked spontaneously, whereas she wrote the post-composition with the organization in mind. However, her attention to the organization did not result in better organization score for the post-composition. Another student reported that she attempted to make the three-part organization of introduction, discussion and conclusion in her post-composition but could not complete the conclusion due to time shortage. It probably took those students who tried to utilize the knowledge more time to write the post-compositions. This probably led them to finish without a concluding statement or with an incomplete one. Furthermore, this could have accounted for the significantly reduced number of total words in the post-compositions. Students' awareness of trying to use the learned knowledge may have hindered the same level of writing fluency they demonstrated in the pre-compositions. If they thought of applying such rules as starting a paragraph with a topic sentence or using transition words while writing, they might have gone through a cognitively more demanding task of sentence production than in the pre-composition time. This could have led to an unfinished composition under the limited time (recall a weak writer's unfinished post-composition quoted above). In order to use the knowledge not so consciously, students probably need to accumulate more writing practice. Nevertheless, their conscious attempt to utilize their knowledge may be a necessary, if not a sufficient, step to using it automatically while writing.

Comparisons of the two groups found that good writers tended to perceive the instruction effects on their writing more highly than did weak writers. Differences in the two groups' perceptions seem to have derived from their consciousness of how much they made use of the learned knowledge while writing post-compositions. More specifically, 6 out of 7 good writers reported their post-compositions reflected the learned knowledge to some degree; whereas 4 of the weak writers claimed they could not make use of it, and the other 3 mentioned they tried to make use of it, but could not do so sufficiently. Two of them pointed out that lack of vocabulary or lexical control in English hindered them from utilizing the knowledge while writing, whereas no good writers mentioned this vocabulary problem. Unlike the good writers, the weak writers could not afford to make full use of the knowledge of paragraph organization presumably because they were tied up with lexical search or syntactic processing in English (recall low-proficiency students' L2 writing processes in Chapter 2). Another possible reason was the time shortage. Because the learned knowledge was closely related to the organization of their writing, their self-evaluations were right in assuming that organization did not improve regardless of the instruction given.

On the other hand, the good writers did not improve their organization in spite of their concern with organization, unity or coherence while writing. Why were there gaps between students' perceptions and composition scores? Three of the good writers claimed that they could not successfully apply the gained knowledge under the time pressure. They found the post-composition time condition far less sufficient. Because the limit was the same for the two conditions, their mention about the time shortage for the post-composition may explain why they reduced the number of words. One of these good writers reported that because her attempt to incorporate the learned knowledge contributed to time problems, she feared that she probably had made many grammatical mistakes. Another good writer reported that she paid attention to the three-part organization (i.e., stating the opinion, presenting supporting reasons, and making concluding remarks), but time ran out when she was writing the concluding sentence. The good writer whose pre- and post-compositions were quoted in the *Research Question 2* section stated that she devoted considerable thought to organizing in both compositions, suggesting both inductive and deductive patterns were consciously organized. She also found the post-composition time particularly short because she attempted to incorporate what she learned into the composition, which led to a short composition.

These reports implied that using the knowledge about English paragraph required a great deal of attention, and even the good writers had not yet developed much faculty to use the learned knowledge under the time pressure. In terms of scores, the good writers did not improve their writing. However, the instruction seems to have exerted inevitable influences on their writing. These students' reflective reports suggest we may need better means to measure effects of instruction. It seems unlikely that the instruction did not help the good writers at all. With more ample time, the knowledge might have been better used and might have improved their writing.

In sum, the two groups' reports showed differences between them. The weak writers had difficulty with lexical retrieval so that they could not afford to use the learned knowledge, whereas the good writers paid attention to the knowledge and took time to use it. With regard to the former finding, weak writers need to make lexical retrieval or syntactic processing automatic. Regarding the latter finding, it should be noted that the high students in Parts I and II had procedurized knowledge of organizational structure in English (i.e., position-statement, its justification, and summary statement). For example, recall Jiro commented that in L2 he had a concluding paragraph almost automatically in the end. Unlike the high students, the good writers in this chapter may still learn to automatize using it. However, it is questionable to compare the findings because the writing conditions were different. The students in Parts I and II had roughly 30 minutes to write in an out-of-class situation, whereas students in Chapter 5 were strictly given only 20 minutes to write as part of an end-of-semester examination.

The results of the present chapter suggest that formal instruction on English paragraph writing can influence student subsequent L2 writing and such an instruction can exert differential influences on students with different L2 writing abilities. On the other hand, findings relating to the possible limitations of formal paragraph instruction are also compelling. The students' overwhelming tendency to present their positions in the initial position, or to use such transition words as "first" and "second," in the post-compositions may raise the question of desirability of molding them to follow a predetermined uniform organizational pattern. After all, as found in Part I, there was no relation between organization patterns and evaluation of organization quality. The present chapter suggests that the testing situation might have pressed the participants to employ the learned pattern. L2 writers can make decisions on how to organize his/her text depending on the writing context. Thus, extending organization repertoire at their disposal is desirable. It is expected that in due course students learn to make choices which type of organization to take or whether to use transition words when enumerating items.

Chapter 5 included not only comparisons of pre- and post-composition scores but also the students' self-evaluations of their pre- and post-compositions in its analysis. By incorporating students' evaluations, the analysis of teaching effects on student writing provided important information that was not captured by analysis of scores alone. Students' own perceptions regarding the instructional effects should be addressed in further studies.

Chapter 6
Writing Strategies and Journal Writing Experience

This chapter reports the effects of teaching writing strategies and journal writing assignments.[1] Unlike in Chapter 5, L2 writing instruction/experience reported in this chapter extended to beyond a paragraph-level, because the students wrote not only multiple drafts for a final paper but also journal entries regularly throughout a course. Writing strategy instruction was meant to include the two essential components of process approach to writing, *"awareness* and *intervention"* (Susser, 1994, p. 34). In other words, attempts were made to build students' awareness of writing processes and to intervene in their writing processes, including prewriting and postwriting, in various ways.

Combining writing strategy instruction with journal writing assignments was made, (a) because Japanese students lack not only writing strategy instruction but also English writing experience, and (b) because the students who received teaching of knowledge about English writing and the journal writing assignments significantly improved the mechanics of their L2 writing, whereas the students who received knowledge-only instruction did not improve their L2 writing significantly (Hirose & Sasaki, 2000). The primary goal of implementing journal writing in the course was to let students get used to writing in English, because this seemed an immediate necessity for inexperienced Japanese writers of English. Journal writing is an individual student activity and is not generally considered a major component of a writing course. For example, journal writing is used "as a supplementary exercise, not as the main activity in any language course" (McCornick, 1993, p. 17) in a Japanese university.

Journal Writing Experience

In L2 writing instruction, journal writing is generally considered more conducive to fluency-aimed writing than to such prewriting activities for generating ideas as proposed in L1 English writing pedagogy. Journal is usually used for writing about personal feelings and experiences in an EFL writing class. Japanese students are generally accustomed to writing about their personal experiences and feelings in their L1, so they can be expected to find little difficulty in adapting themselves to journal writing in an L2 (see Liebman, 1992).

Fluency-aimed writing practice, such as journal writing or fast writing, has been implemented in Japanese university classrooms, not on a massive scale yet, but enough so that a few empirical studies have reported on its use. The effects of this type of writing practice have already been examined and reported. First, because students are writing in a non-threatening environment, they experience less anxiety about writing and become more comfortable with writing in English (Kresovich, 1988). Probably related to this 'ease' effect, students have also gained writing fluency. Measuring fluency by the number of T-units and words, for example, Ross, Shortreed, and Robb (1988) found that students became more fluent in writing, especially in narrative writing, over a 1-year writing course. This increase in fluency may be caused by changes in students' writing processes, for example, from a word-for-word translation from Japanese to English to direct writing in English. Although writing fluency has been an established effect, past studies have reported mixed results concerning the effects of journal writing on writing quality (e.g., Ross et al., 1988). For example, Casanave (1994) reported conflicting results during an 18-month journal writing experience. Two thirds of her Japanese university students improved their writing, but not all students produced longer, more complex sentences or more accurate language use. Therefore, the effects of fluency-aimed writing experience on writing quality should be examined more fully.

Despite its expected effects, spontaneous writing such as free or journal writing does not require writers to do much planning beforehand. Furthermore, while writing, they do not have to, and are actually instructed not to, worry about coherence or organization either. Common sense dictates that coherent, well-organized writing does not come naturally from such fluent writing alone. This is where writing strategy instruction comes into play.

Writing Strategy Instruction

As found in Part II of the present volume, L2 good and weak writers differed in terms of writing strategies they used while writing. For example, good writers tended to make a global plan to which they adhered while writing, whereas weak writers had a tendency to plan what to write next. The former were concerned about appropriateness of language they were about to produce or had written down, whereas the latter mostly cared about the surface forms such as spelling or grammar. Such writing strategies as global planning (**Pp**), refining rhetoric (**L**), and reader consciousness (**Lc**) that only good writers tended to use should be taught to inexperienced writers like the low students in Part II.

Unlike teaching knowledge about English paragraphs reported in

Chapter 5, L2 writing strategy instruction has not yet found its place in Japan. A cross-country survey of tertiary English writing teachers' views and practices in the Asia-Pacific region, including five countries/regions, found that teachers in Japan were the most product-oriented in terms of theory and practice, and made the least use of process-oriented procedures among those teachers surveyed (Pennington, Costa, So, Shing, Hirose, & Niedzielski, 1997). Published coursebooks made for teaching writing strategies were not so widely available as those for teaching English paragraphs, and no textbooks were used for this course. Instead, I chose and adapted some activities from Littlejohn (1991; 1994) for writing strategy instruction (see the Content of Instruction section for details). In order to connect such writing strategy instruction with students' own writing, I set a final goal of writing a research paper by the end of the semester, so that the students could experience multi-draft writing before the completion of the final draft.

Thus, the effects of teaching writing strategies and writing experience are investigated in this chapter. I specifically examine whether and how such instruction/writing experience actually affects students' writing processes as well as writing products. Furthermore, the present chapter attempts to explore whether there are any particular characteristics of those students who show improvement in terms of their writing process. The results of Chapter 5 revealed that the effects of instruction differed according to the individual student. Some gained higher scores after the instruction, whereas others did not. Those results of Chapter 5 suggest students' initial L2 writing ability can be a factor that determines improvement. It was the weak writers who gained points for the post-composition. In this chapter, therefore, I try to uncover process characteristics that pertain to such "successful" students who gained points.

Research Questions

The present chapter explores three research questions:

1. Does instruction of writing strategies combined with journal writing experience have an effect on Japanese students' L2 writing?
2. Does this combined instruction have an effect on Japanese students' L2 writing processes?
3. Are there any characteristics in common among those who improve their writing?

Method

Participants

A total of 23 Japanese university students (4 men and 19 women) taking a course titled "English Composition I" at a public university day school participated in the present segment of the study. As in the case of the participants in Chapter 5, this was the first English composition course they took at the university. Participant English proficiency, based on the CELT Form A, varied from low-intermediate to advanced, with the majority of these students belonging to the intermediate level (see Table 33). On average, their L2 proficiency level was higher than that of the participants in Chapter 5 (CELT total score mean=180.4; CELT total score range: 121-264).[2]

Table 33: Descriptive Statistics of Participants' CELT Scores (N=23)

Measure (total possible)	M	SD	Range
CELT Listening (100)	72.8	13.2	48 - 96
CELT Structure (100)	81.4	7.6	65 - 93
CELT Vocabulary (100)	56.3	11.4	44 - 81
CELT Total (300)	210.5	24.3	172-264

Content of Instruction

(1) Journal Writing Assignments

The students were told to write a diary entry at least 4 days a week outside the class throughout the course. In addition to instructions such as "Spend no fewer than 15 minutes when writing," "Try to write as much as you can about anything," and "Do not worry too much about spelling and grammar," they were told that only the amount of writing would be taken into consideration for grading this practice.

The subject of journal writing was mostly concerned with what students did in a day and what they thought or felt about these experiences. Thus, common topics were about university courses they were taking, including professors, classmates, tests or assignments; part-time jobs they did after classes; and social activities they engaged in outside of class. As many students complained that they could not think of a topic because they followed a similar routine every day, I suggested possible topics at times, but some students always explored their own ideas.

For journal writing, a journal check form was prepared every week in which students filled in the number of lines for each entry for a week, the day they chose for a reader to read, and a blank column for questions or comments from the reader. The reader wrote several English sentences in the column freely. They spent approximately 10-15 minutes of the class time reading and giving written feedback to each other. This in-class activity was intended to ensure regular writing and raise students' awareness of audience when they did journal writing.

During the 12-week course, on average, the participants in this chapter wrote 933 lines (of more than 6 words each). In other words, they wrote 77.8 lines (approximately 5 pages) in a week.

(2) Writing Strategy Instruction through Research Paper Writing

The writing strategy instruction consisted of three components: (a) consciousness toward students' writing and writing processes were raised; (b) writing strategies, especially those used by good writers were explicitly taught; and (c) opportunities to use such strategies were given.

First, prior student knowledge/experience of writing was elicited through such questions as "What do you think of writing?" (adapted from Unit 5 in Littlejohn, 1994). Students seemed to share the view that writing was not always easy even in an L1, and they were especially anxious about formal writing. For example, they described L1 writing as "easier than English," "troublesome," or "difficult." Then I asked such additional questions as "What makes writing difficult?," "Do you have the same feelings about L2 writing?," and "What is good L1 and L2 writing?" Consequently, different perceptions or ideas about writing emerged. For example, students considered good writing as being clear in the sense that the reader finds it easy to follow, in both the L1 and L2. On the other hand, students had split opinions about good L1 and L2 writing. Some students argued that they should quickly "get to the point" when writing in English. On the other hand, others claimed English and Japanese were basically the same. Acknowledging there was a perception by English readers that Japanese writing is indirect, I gave students an illustration of such writing and showed them Kaplan's (1966) diagram (Figure 2). Nevertheless, I also added that Japanese writers can be logical both in English and in Japanese (recall discussion in Chapter 1).

I also held class discussion on multi-draft writing processes, from generating ideas to revising. More specifically, students drew a chart of their writing processes in a group (adapted from Unit 5 in Littlejohn, 1994), and then each group reporter presented the chart visually and orally to the whole class. The charts or diagrams the students completed in each group were not exactly the same, but they shared some common features including the recursive (nonlinear) nature of writing. After eliciting from students their own views of academic writing processes, I proceeded to ask whether paper writing processes in English would be the same as those in Japanese. Student consciousness of L1/L2 academic writing processes was raised because, at first, many students tended to regard the two processes as totally different. Therefore, I focused on similarities in L1/L2 writing processes, for instance, prewriting research activities such as outlining, rewriting, and revising. In this way, students' awareness of writing process was heightened through explanation and discussions in the whole class.

Regarding strategy instruction, the main point was to introduce several writing strategies to serve a purpose, for example, for global planning. Unlike the case of journal writing, the importance of planning and postwriting activities was emphasized for research paper writing to be done. Such prewriting activities as free writing and outlining (e.g., making a list or drawing tree diagrams) were demonstrated, then the students tried them. More specifically, they had 10-15 minutes of hands-on experience with each of two types of prewriting activities (adapted from Unit 15 in Littlejohn, 1991). The intention was to enhance students' awareness of different approaches to getting started with writing and to let them discover which approach would suit them best. The students chose topics on their own for these activities, as well as for their papers. After they did these activities, most participants reported they preferred outlining to free writing as an idea-generating activity. With still limited experience of journal writing, they appeared as yet unable to translate the activity into an idea-generating prewriting activity. This may be attributable not only to their lack of L2 writing experience and/or L2 proficiency, but also to individual preferences (i.e., either "brainstormer" or "outliner"; see Reid, 1984).

Regarding planning, the importance of organizing ideas was also emphasized. Students were instructed to include in their own research papers the three main sections (i.e., introduction, body, and conclusion), each of whose functions was explained explicitly. They were also instructed to do global planning, i.e., to plan the main points and their sequence for the body of the paper. When they announced to the whole class their topics, they presented brief outlines and the reasons for their choice orally in English. Then, students worked on their own projects, starting with generating ideas and organizing them in the form of lists. They all handed in an outline of their papers, which was commented on and returned, before they began to write. Students did independent research activities such as reading and conducting a survey before writing their papers. After summarizing their findings based on their survey or reading, they began writing their first drafts mostly as homework assignments, which were then read and commented on by me and other students in the class. Both teacher and peer feedback was used to raise reader consciousness while writing, another good writers' strategy. I gave both spoken and written feedback to the students' drafts individually, whereas students exchanged written feedback with each other in class. Based on teacher and peer feedback, students were encouraged to revise the drafts and then produce better papers for grading by the end of the semester (see Hirose, 2001, for more details of teacher-student conferences and peer feedback used in the course).

They were also required to type English on a word processor or personal computer. For many students, this was their first serious attempt to type in English. Getting used to a computer made their rewriting and revising easier. In the last class, students made oral presentations in English on their projects and handed in their research papers. The course, therefore, included many process writing pedagogies such as journal writing, teacher/student conferences, peer feedback, and revising (Susser, 1994).

Data

(1) Pre- and Post-Instruction Compositions

The participants wrote a 30-minute English composition at the beginning and at the end of the course.[3] For the pre-instruction composition, the following prompt was given in L1:

> In the readers' column in an English newspaper, there has been a heated discussion about the issue of "women and work." Some people think that women should continue to work even after they get married, whereas others believe they should stay at home and take care of their families after marriage. Now the editor of the newspaper is calling for the readers' opinions. Suppose you are writing for the readers' opinion column. Take one of the positions described above, and write your opinion.

At the end of the course, they wrote another English composition given the following prompt in L1:

> In the readers' column in an English newspaper, there has been a heated discussion about the issue of "university students and part-time jobs." Some people think that students should not have part-time jobs, whereas others believe they should work part-time. Now the editor of the newspaper is calling for the readers' opinions. Suppose you are writing for the readers' opinion column. Take one of the positions described above, and write your opinion.

As in Chapter 5, both compositions were scored by two English L2 writing specialists, according to Jacobs et al.'s (1981) ESL Composition Profile. Ratings were assigned for the five criteria of <u>content</u>, <u>organization</u>, <u>language use</u>, <u>vocabulary</u>, and <u>mechanics</u>. Each participant's composition score was the sum of the two raters' scores, with a possible range from 68 to 200 points. In addition, the total number of words per composition was also counted.

(2) Postwriting Questionnaire on Writing Processes

Pre- and post-composition tasks were immediately followed by a postwriting questionnaire designed to examine how participants produced their compositions (see Appendix I). It asked (a) whether they did any prewriting activities, and if they did, what kind of things they did; (b) how they kept writing, whether they translated or wrote directly in English, or what they did when they got stuck while writing; (c) how much attention they paid to <u>grammar</u>, <u>spelling</u>, <u>content</u>, <u>overall organization</u>, and <u>vocabulary choice</u> (measured by a 5-point Likert scale); and (d) what they did after writing.

Data Analysis

For *Research Question 1*, the pre- and post-compositions of all participating students were compared in terms of the five subscores, total scores, and total number of words using paired *t*-tests. Because 6 comparisons were made for L2 composition scores, I accepted only those *t*-tests that were below the 0.0083 level as significant. For *Research Question 2*, each postwriting questionnaire item except rating of attention was tested using McNemar's test for the significance of changes between pre- and post-composition writing. Regarding how much attention they paid to grammar, spelling, content, overall organization, and vocabulary choice while writing, self-rating of pre- and post-compositions were compared using paired *t*-tests. For *Research Question 3*, the participants who gained scores for post-composition were chosen to determine what characteristics they had.

Results and Discussion

Research Question 1: Comparisons of Pre- and Post-Instruction Compositions

Table 34 displays descriptive statistics for the total scores, the five subscores, and the total words of the pre- and post-compositions. Reliability estimates for the composition scores are interrater reliability estimates based on Pearson correlation coefficients. As shown in Table 34, reliability estimates for the composition scores were generally high except for the post-composition vocabulary (0.48) and mechanics (0.36). Thus, the results concerning these two subscores should be treated with caution.

As Table 34 shows, the students gained scores in all measures. However, results of paired *t*-tests revealed that there were no significant differences in any subscore or total score. After the instruction, the students did not significantly improve their writing. Judging from their pre-composition scores, the participants were relatively good writers before they took the L2 writing instruction. Their L2 writing level corresponded to that of the high students in Parts I and II of the present volume (recall Table 5 for their L2 composition scores). As discussed in Chapter 5, it might not be easy for good writers to further improve their writing especially in the limited period of time like a 12-week course.

Table 34: Descriptive Statistics of Pre- and Post-Instruction Composition Scores (*N*=23)

Measure (total possible)	Pre-Instruction			Post-Instruction		
	M	*SD*	Reliability	*M*	*SD*	Reliability
Comp. Total (200)	150.39	14.67	0.88	156.35	12.19	0.69
Content (60)	48.48	4.09	0.79	49.91	3.55	0.70
Organization (40)	31.70	3.04	0.73	32.35	2.99	0.58
Vocabulary (40)	29.17	2.89	0.72	30.65	2.44	0.48
Language Use (50)	32.70	5.81	0.62	34.57	3.87	0.66
Mechanics (10)	8.35	0.89	0.64	8.87	0.97	0.36
Total No. of Words	157.5	50.6	—	220.1	55.6	—

Only the total number of words was found to be significantly different (*t*=-7.1, *p*<.0001). The post-compositions were longer than the pre-compositions by 62.6 words (i.e., 39.7% increase) on average. Because the 200–300 word length was given as an acceptable level for ESL compositions written in 30 minutes (Jacobs et al., 1981), it is possible to claim that the students had reached that acceptable level in terms of writing quantity. Thus, the quantity increase without the sacrifice of quality can be considered the major effect of the present instruction. Good writers are those who can write quickly and fluently. As pointed out in Part II, however, a large quantity was not necessarily related to good quality of writing. This was exemplified by the most productive writer in both pre- and post-compositions in the present chapter. She produced 333 words and 423 words in her pre- and post-composition, respectively, both exceeding the group means. Although her pre-composition scored higher than the group mean, her post-composition score was the lowest in the group.

The post-compositions were not significantly different from the pre-compositions in any of the criteria examined, but the finding of significantly longer post-compositions may suggest that this combination of L2 writing instruction posits good signs of potentiality. It is particularly worthy of attention in connection with the significant result concerning composition length in Chapter 5. That is, the participants in the previous chapter wrote significantly shorter compositions after the instruction. They reduced writing quantity without the sacrifice of quality. Because the pre- and post-writing tasks including times and instructional content were different in the two cases, we should be cautious to compare the results. Nevertheless, it can be speculated that the present chapter's participants' extensive writing practice contributed to improvement in quantity of argumentative writing. In relation to this finding, recall that Ross et al.'s (1988) participants who did journal writing increased the number of words in narrative writing. It is difficult, however, to determine conclusively which component, writing strategy instruction with paper writing experience or journal writing experience, was more effective in improving writing fluency while maintaining a certain level of writing quality.

Lastly, I should take Susser's (1994) criticism against assessing writing product using Jacobs et al.'s (1981) scale after process-oriented writing instruction because the scale was not designed to assess writing process (see the Summary of Part III section for the needs for other assessment measures).

Research Question 2: Comparisons of Pre- and Post-Instruction Writing Processes

McNemar's tests did not indicate any significant change in any item examined. For example, Table 35 summarizes the students' responses to a question item "Did you start writing right away?" (see Appendix I). It shows that 8 students started writing without any planning in the pre-composition, and half of those students did not do so in the post-composition. Conversely, 15 students did some prewriting activities in the pre-composition, whereas 9 of those students did not do so in the post-composition. Comparing the students' responses between pre- and post-composition times, 10 students (43.5%) did not differ, whereas 13 students (56.5%) differed in terms of how they started writing. The McNemar's analysis checked if these changes between the two writing times were significant statistically. The results found no significant changes in any of the questionnaire items examined. The analyzed responses included such items as translating generated ideas into English, direct writing in English, writing with the overall

Table 35: Students' Responses to the Question "Did you start writing right away?"

		Pre-Instruction		
		Yes	No	
Post-Instruction	Yes	4	9	13
	No	4	6	10
		8	15	23

organization in mind, or writing spontaneously (see Appendix I, Part II, Question 1).

On the other hand, regarding how much attention they paid to various aspects while writing, the students rated differently between pre- and post-compositions in 2 out of 5 items (see Appendix I, Part II, Question 2). According to the t-test results, they directed significantly more attention to content and overall organization while writing post-compositions. In writing pre-compositions, they rated the <u>organization</u> at an average of 2.61 in the 5-point Likert scale, whereas they rated it at 3.35 in post-compositions ($t=-4.4, p<0.001$). Another significant difference was found in their attention to <u>content</u> (pre-composition mean=3.26; post-composition mean=3.74; $t=-3.2, p<0.005$). On average, they paid exactly the same amount of attention to <u>vocabulary choice</u> (mean=2.83), <u>grammar</u> (mean=2.87), and <u>spelling</u> (mean=2.83) while writing pre- and post-compositions. Thus, the results showed that they drew more attention to content and overall organization while writing post-compositions. They could afford to be concerned with these probably because they did not require much attention to linguistic operations such as spelling, syntactic processing, and vocabulary choice.

It would have taken more than the given time to see the effects of teaching on students' use of writing strategies. For example, even though students had learned brainstorming and listing as prewriting activities, they could hardly exercise brainstorming to its fulfillment especially in timed writing. In fact, 5 participants (21.7%) in the present chapter reported that when they finished writing their post-compositions, they did not have time to reread or revise because the time had elapsed. Even if they learned rereading or revising was important through their paper writing experience, they simply could not put it into practice. Thus, the effects of writing strategy instruction can be hard to see in the timed writing situation such as used in the present study. Therefore, in order to investigate whether students are constrained from using some writing strategies under time pressure, we should provide time-free writing conditions to students, and then compare their writing processes, as in Bereiter and Scardamalia (1987). Furthermore, examination of writing strategies in use is harder than assessment of product. It is even harder to determine whether change in process actually leads to product improvement.

Research Question 3: Characteristics of Writing Processes when Writing Improved

(1) The Relation between Writing Strategy Use and Product

Considering the pre- and postwriting processes were not significantly different except in terms of their attention paid to content and organization while writing, individual students' writing processes are examined in this section to explore whether the use of certain writing strategies resulted in improvement. Then, those students who increased scores for the post-composition are focused on in order to capture what characteristics they have.

Using good writers' writing strategies did not necessarily lead the students to produce good quality writing (see Pennington & So, 1993, for similar findings). For example, the student who scored the least in the group and actually decreased the most (23 points) in the post-composition went through the writing processes we would expect good writers to typically have recourse to. Before writing her post-composition, she planned content and overall organization. While writing, she paid attention to the overall organization very much and tried to write a coherent composition by thinking of the connection between sentences.

She rated 5 (very) for <u>overall organization</u> in a 5-point Likert scale. After writing, she reread the composition to find spelling mistakes and also added what she found missing to it.

On the other hand, those students who did not pay attention to organization scored better. In contrast to the student who scored the least, the student who gained the highest score (34 points) for the post-composition only thought of content before writing and was not so concerned about organization while writing. He rated 2 (little) for <u>overall organization</u>. After writing his post-composition, he checked spelling and grammar. Furthermore, his writing processes did not differ much between his pre-composition and post-composition. Regardless of the non-use of good writers' strategies and little change in the two writing processes, he scored much better in his post-composition.

A more notable example of little change between the two processes and non-use of good writers' strategies was the student who scored the top in both pre- and post-compositions in the present chapter. In the postwriting questionnaires, she responded she started writing right away and wrote directly in English without considering overall organization at all in both compositions. In fact, she rated 1 (not at all) for <u>overall organization</u> in a 5-point Likert scale, the least of the five points given. She paid the least attention to the organization while writing both compositions. Her pre-composition organization score was the top, and the post-composition score was the second top in the group. After she finished writing, furthermore, she reread her pre-composition to see if she had made spelling mistakes, and in her post-composition she was concerned about grammar mistakes as well as spelling mistakes. Writing without planning, continuing to write with little concern about the overall organization, and only rereading for the surface forms such as spelling and grammar are what characterize weak writers, rather than good writers.

Nevertheless, her two compositions were evaluated most highly, respectively. Her case clearly shows that a good writing product does not directly result from using good writers' writing strategies.

Thus, as far as the results of the present chapter are concerned, there seems to be no causal relation between strategy use and product.

(2) Characteristics of those Students who Improved their Writing

Examinations of pre- and postwriting processes in the *Research Question 2* section disclosed no significant differences between the two except in the degree of attention paid to several aspects while writing. In this section, comparisons between the pre- and postwriting processes are made within the "successful" participants in terms of writing quality.

In order to capture characteristics of those who improved their writing, those students who increased 20 or more total points for the post-composition were chosen for the analysis in this section. Those 4 students who gained 20 or more points turned out to have increased 108 total words, on average. Furthermore, for the pre-composition 3 of them had scored 135 points or less, scores which were 1 *SD* below the group mean of 150.39. The fourth student had scored 142 points, which, although higher than the other 3 students, was nevertheless also below the group mean. Although these "successful" students may not be categorized as weak EFL writers based on their final scores (their post-composition mean=160.25), they belonged to the weak writer group in the present study due to their initial scores (their pre-composition mean=134.25). In contrast, those students who had pre-composition scores more than 1 *SD* above the mean (166 and more) turned out to have decreased on average 8.67 points for the post-composition. Although these good writers (3 students) still wrote better and longer post-compositions than the "successful" students, they did not display much difference in terms of the total scores between the pre- and post-compositions. Thus, it seems the weak writers, rather than the good writers, showed substantial improvement in terms of numerical indices of writing quality and quantity.

These 4 students who substantially improved their writing quality are focused on in this section, and their postwriting questionnaire responses are compared between the pre- and postwriting times individually. The results showed that all of these "successful" students only had one process feature in common. That is, all of them wrote what they thought directly in English while writing the pre-composition. This is, however, not specific to these "successful" students because 91.3% of the whole group reported having done so. None of the 4 students reported having translated into L2 sentence by sentence while writing the pre- and post-compositions. This is also not restricted to the "successful" students. No single process factor examined in the present section was found to be commonly attributable to improvement. For example, greater attention paid to various aspects of writing seemed to help some "successful" writers to improve their writing in the post-composition time. On the other hand, greater attention to such aspects as spelling and vocabulary choice seemed to stifle one "successful" student's fluent writing. Less attention drawn to those aspects in her post-composition process seemed to help her improve her writing fluency and also her writing quality. As the analysis in this section implied, each student's somewhat differing process features contributed to the diverse findings in the present chapter. Various factors were entangled with the improvement in quality and quantity, even within a single writer. Thus, examining changes in the writing process may require more in-depth data such as interview data from the participants.

Summary of Part III

Part III of the present study has reported effects of two types of English writing instruction on the Japanese university students' subsequent writing. The results of Chapter 5 revealed the following.
1. The teaching of English organization had some effects on Japanese university students' L2 writing significantly, but it had little effect on the improvement of organization.
2. The teaching effects appeared to differ according to students' L2 writing ability; it was the weak writers who improved their writing.
3. The participating students shared perceptions of the teaching effects in the sense that they were keen to use the learned knowledge while writing but that they could not do so to their fulfillment.

Although the small sample size may limit the generalizability of the results, overall the study found positive effects of teaching English paragraph organization. By incorporating students' self-reports into its investigation, Chapter 5 attempted to uncover students' own perceptions of the post-compositions in comparison with their pre-compositions. The students' reports revealed that they were keen to use the knowledge about English paragraphs while writing post-compositions, although this did not result in better organization in terms of scores. Nevertheless, their reports suggest that students may well have been making progress in organizational skills, which might also account for the reduced number of the total words. In this sense, the reduced number may be one of the best indices that the instruction worked well with the students. Although the validity of the students' self-evaluation should be tested against their compositions, the present study found it roughly to correspond to their compositions. The students thought the post-compositions were better than the pre-compositions, with reservations about the manifestation of the learned knowledge. If the practice time was not sufficient to improve students' organization, they would need more writing practice in applying the knowledge. Furthermore, the issue of transferability of L2 writing knowledge in both L2 and L1 writing needs to be explored in further studies. Miyata (1994) found that English paragraph writing instruction exerted various effects on junior college students' L1 Japanese writing, and suggests that L2 paragraph writing instruction improves the logic of L1 Japanese composition too.*

Subsequently, Chapter 6 revealed the following.
1. The instruction of writing strategy with journal writing experience did not have significant effects on the quality of student writing, but it had significant effects on the improvement of writing quantity.
2. The teaching did not have effects enough to influence their writing processes.
3. The good writers' strategy use did not seem to be a factor that determined writing quality.
4. The teaching effects differed relative to students' writing ability; the weak writers tended to improve their writing after the instruction.

Although such writing strategies as planning both content and organization, paying attention to organization, rereading and revising were taught explicitly and experienced through paper writing process, the students did not necessarily use these strategies while writing post-compositions. As the top student's writing processes depicted above showed, there seems to be no point to trace features that led her to produce good writing product from her responses to the postwriting questionnaire items. Inversely, the student who scored the least used strategies that characterized good writers. Furthermore, there were few differences between the pre- and postwriting processes, although different topics could have affected their strategy use (Carter, 1990).

These findings may cast doubt on the effectiveness of writing strategy instruction. Horowitz (1986) warned against process pedagogies in that they would not help students to prepare for such academic writing as examination. Nevertheless, it is too early to conclude that this type of L2 writing instruction

---

*I owe the information about Miyata (1994) to Hashiuchi (1995).

does not help develop argumentative writing ability. Process pedagogies now constitute part of ESL academic writing courses (Goldstein, 1993) and are considered helpful for academic writing (Susser, 1994). It would have taken the participants more than a semester to learn to use writing strategies in their own writing. In fact, Sasaki (2000) reported that 6-month process writing instruction did not significantly improve EFL Japanese students' writing quality and quantity, with the reservation that such instruction "may have the potential to improve students' L2 writing" (p. 272). Thus, we should further examine whether explicitly taught strategies such as global planning are actually transferred to writing processes and reflected in end-products (i.e., better organized compositions), and whether L2 writing strategies learned through such instruction are transferable/transferred to L1 writing. In L1, Smagorinsky (1991) examined the effects of teaching brainstorming or revising strategies on the writing processes of student writers by using protocol analysis. In contrast, few empirical studies have been conducted on the effects of writing strategy instruction on L2 writers. Thus, we should further investigate longitudinally if and how the explicit L2 writing instruction and writing experience will affect students' writing processes by using a more direct method such as protocol analysis (see Smagorinsky, 1991, for L1 study).

Related to the pedagogical implications, appropriate methods of teaching writing strategies need more elaboration. The writing course described in Chapter 6 was my attempt to include writing strategy instruction in English writing instruction, and changes/improvements need to be made for more classroom use. Scardamalia, Bereiter, and Steinbach (1984) reported L1 writing instruction using a list of cues that stimulated self-questioning during planning, and found some change reflected in students' writing processes (see also Bereiter & Scardamalia, 1987). In order to propose such methods, we need to further examine what strategies L2 expert writers use. The good writers in the present study were not highly experienced or expert writers.

Regarding student subsequent writing, Chapters 5 and 6 in the present volume have yielded similar, and somewhat different, findings in terms of writing quality. In both chapters, the participants improved their subsequent writing, although not significantly, in terms of overall quality represented in the total scores. On the other hand, those participants in Chapter 5 improved mechanics and vocabulary significantly, whereas those in Chapter 6 did not show significant improvement in any item examined. The differences in these results of the two chapters can be attributed to different levels of L2 proficiency/writing ability at the time instruction started. More specifically, those in Chapter 6 had higher L2 proficiency/writing levels than those in Chapter 5. Compare the two participant groups' CELT scores (Tables 29 and 33) and pre- and post-composition mean scores (Tables 30 and 34). Every mean score of those participants in Chapter 6 was higher than that in Chapter 5. The present study revealed students with lower levels of L2 proficiency/writing ability seem to have shown improvement more significantly. Furthermore, mechanics may be one of the first items that show the effects of instruction or practice (see Hirose & Sasaki, 2000, for a similar finding). The results of the present research also suggest use of vocabulary as well as skills regarding punctuation or paragraphing may be learned early compared with other skills concerning language use and organization.

In terms of writing quantity, Chapters 5 and 6 reported conflicting results concerning student subsequent writing. Those in Chapter 6 increased, but those in Chapter 5 decreased, the writing quantity. More interestingly, these contrastive findings regarding quantity were both regarded as positive effects of instruction, respectively. As discussed in Part I, the relation between writing quantity and quality is complicated, and thus an increase or a decrease in words cannot be considered either positive or negative in its own light.

The studies conducted in Part III would need to be extended to a larger sample size to validate its findings with other student populations. A similar type of instruction can also be given, and its effects can be tested at the high school level, too. In particular, the finding that the weak writers in Part III improved their writing in several ways may encourage such implementation. Follow-up studies should also be conducted to examine the effects of English writing instruction longer than a semester and/or with the use of more paragraph- and essay-level writing practice.

Lastly, students' improvement in writing should be measured over a longer term. The present study has only examined the students' subsequent writing after the two types of instruction. As Leki (1990) has pointed out, "there is little information on long-term improvement in writing" (p. 58). I have measured their improvements in terms of writing quantity (in terms of the number of words produced under the set time) and writing quality (evaluated by analytical writing scale). Over a longer term, however, there should be ways other than numerical tools to examine students' improvement as L2 writers. For example, they may change their attitude toward writing (preferably may become less negative, lower their anxiety toward writing, or become more motivated to write in L2). These affective or attitudinal factors should also be included in further studies.

Conclusion

Parts I and II of the present volume have explored the relationship between L1 and L2 writing by integrating writing product and process data collected from two different L2 proficiency groups of EFL Japanese students. The study revealed that: (a) despite the stereotypical view that Japanese prefer an inductive type pattern, a majority of the participants in the present study employed a deductive type pattern both in L1 and L2, particularly in L2; (b) low L2 proficiency students produced L1/L2 compositions with similar organizational patterns by going through different writing processes from each other, whereas high-proficiency students tended to organize L1/L2 compositions differently resorting to similar writing processes; (c) despite the similarities revealed in the quantitative analysis of L1/L2 writing processes, the qualitative analysis found the participants' L1/L2 writing processes were different in several ways; (d) the two groups of students employed some similar writing strategies, whereas each group also relied on other strategies not so frequently used by the other group; and (e) low-proficiency students' L2 writing was impeded by not only limited L2 proficiency but also non-use of good writers' writing strategies, whereas high students compensated for their less skilled L2 writing (as compared to L1 writing) with more detailed planning and controlling their writing based on their plans.

These results should be treated with caution because the sample size was small. They should also be interpreted, taking the timed nature of the writing tasks into consideration. Thus, the findings should be confirmed with a larger sample of participants. It is also important to confirm the results with different topics or types of tasks other than argumentative writing in a short period of time. Because the topics of L1/L2 writing tasks were different in the present study, we cannot entirely dismiss the influence of the topic variable on the writers' choice of organizational patterns as well as writing process behaviors. It is equally necessary to extend the study to include different groups of students such as those with higher or lower L2 proficiency levels or expert L2 writers. In contrastive rhetoric research, in particular, the investigation would need to be extended to validate its findings with non-English major Japanese students who have different L1 writing abilities with little background in L2 writing instruction/experience. They may constitute a more appropriate participant group to investigate the effects of L1 writing instruction/experience on L2 writing.

Despite the limitations, the present study suggests several directions for future research as well as implications for writing instruction. First, the relation between L1 and L2 organizational patterns requires further investigation. The results of this study imply that multi-faceted factors are involved in students' choices of L1/L2 organizational patterns. Both writer-related factors such as instructional background and perceptions about good organization and other factors like task (including time) had influences on their choices. Besides conducting large-scale research, it is equally important for studies within the contrastive rhetoric tradition to examine these factors in much greater depth. For example, studies of the effects of L1 writing experience and instruction on L2 writing are required to elucidate whether and how such prior writing experience affects students' choices of essay organization in L2. Those L2 writers who have not yet acquired sufficient organizational ability in L1 argumentative writing may need such writing experience in L1, which can then potentially benefit their L2 argumentative writing. Alternatively, L1 argumentative writing experience may not be a necessary condition for L2 organizational ability to develop. L2 writing instruction and experience may be transferable to L1 writing. These issues remain for further study.

Second, we should also examine the relation between rhetorical patterns and text quality both in L1 and L2. For example, whether a certain type of rhetorical pattern is related to higher quality of Japanese texts or not is still unsolved. Kubota (1998b) suggests that use of inductive style leads to low evaluation in Japanese. The present study, however, did not bear out any such relation between organizational pattern and evaluation, and even speculates that use of inductive style may be associated with good writers' strategies in Japanese. Probably good writers, both in Japanese and English, can choose organization according to topics and readers. Individual readers as well as writers may also favor different patterns. Thus, this issue needs to be examined in future research with a much larger number of raters including students.

Third, regarding the factor of readers, L1 and L2 readers' perceptions of good organization and writing should also be addressed in more in-depth studies. It may be possible to make comparisons between English-speaking and Japanese-speaking readers' perceptions and expectations of argumentative organizations. Both groups may share similar organizational patterns or schema. Such future study will help to contribute to new approaches to contrastive rhetoric research by helping dispel some of the inaccurate overgeneralizations of Japanese and English writing so prevalent in the contrastive rhetoric field.

Regarding writing process research and pedagogy, follow-up studies should also be conducted to examine whether writing processes of novice L2 writers such as the low students in Parts I and II of the present volume change as their L2 proficiency improves or if they take L2 writing instruction and/or accumulate L2 writing experience. If they change their writing processes, how do they change? How does the use of L1 during L2 writing change as they learn to write in L2? Do their L2 writing processes become more similar to those in L1? Longitudinal studies of the same writers should investigate these issues.

With regard to pedagogical implications of Part III of the present volume, the content of L2 writing instruction needs to be further examined and implemented in the classroom. The results of Chapter 5 implied that teaching of knowledge about English paragraphs would facilitate students' use of the knowledge while writing and thus may change their writing processes. Furthermore, the results of Chapter 6 revealed that beyond a paragraph-level writing experience facilitated writing fluency and exerted an influence on their attention to content and organization while writing. The present study also found diversity of writing processes even within a student group with similar L2 proficiency level and L2 writing ability. The variation among the present participants' writing processes suggests that individualization may be desirable in writing instruction. It may be difficult to instruct a contemplator or outliner to put down on paper whatever comes to mind. On the other hand, it is easy for a spontaneous writer or brainstormer to do so, but s/he needs to learn to organize the composition or reread and revise what has already been written. Writing strategy instruction needs more elaboration to adapt to individual differences and needs.

In order to investigate the effects of writing instruction on student writing, it may be necessary to conduct longitudinal studies for a period longer than one semester, for example, over a one-, two-, or three-year period. Such studies will require diverse means to measure teaching effects on students' L2 writing, as suggested by Casanave (1994). Improvement should be assessed in various ways, not solely by numerical indices of writing quality or quantity. For example, affective factors such as motivational and interest levels toward L2 writing can be subject to change as students accumulate writing experience. Thus, further study should follow up not only with a larger sample size quantitative study but also much more detailed case studies in which salient characteristics of those students who improve are uncovered in much greater depth. Such in-depth studies should employ interviews and protocols. These future studies mentioned in this section will complement the pedagogical applications of the present study.

Notes

Chapter 1

1. I owe the information about Leggett (1966; 1975) to Kinoshita (1981).
2. As Figure 2 shows, Kaplan (1966) used the term "Oriental."
3. With regard to L1 reading instruction, both literary and expository passages are included. Thus, Japanese students have experienced reading expository prose at school.
4. Given impetus from U.S. academic rhetorical education, Kinoshita has published guidebooks on how to write a paper in Japanese for science-major university students and adults (1981) and their liberal-arts major counterparts (1990) and has also engaged in developing L1 textbooks for elementary, junior, and senior high school students.
5. When students seek a job after graduation, *shôronbun* is again part of the job-seeking process for employment by both public and private sectors. Thus, guidebooks and practice books on *shôronbun* abound for university students, too.
6. Although the authors used the term *expository writing*, the task required taking a position and supporting it. Kubota (1998b) called a similar task *persuasive writing*. The terms *argumentative* and *persuasive* writing are used interchangeably to refer to this type of writing. In the present study, I use *argumentative writing*.
7. On the other hand, Henry (1993) and the present study are different in many ways. For example, Henry's (1993) participants were highly experienced, some were published, writers in L1 (age range = 24–32), but all from different countries. Their L2 proficiency and L2 writing levels seem to correspond to those of the high group in the present study. The methods of collecting and analyzing data were also different in that Henry (1993) collected think-aloud data, as opposed to the recall data used in the present study. Instead of transcribing the audiotaped data, Henry counted and analyzed composing behaviors directly from the tapes. The present study used transcribed protocol data accompanied with videotaped data.
8. Some could argue that a letter writing task is common for which people receive little or no instruction at school (Hirose, 1990). However, a letter writing task to the paper especially to state and support one's opinion pertains to argumentative writing. It was considered most unlikely that any of the participants had engaged in writing opinion letters to a newspaper editor. Nevertheless, this task was chosen because it provided them probable context for argumentative writing.
9. Some might argue that the 30-minute writing time was not enough to finish to their satisfaction. As summarized by Silva's (1993) survey article, limiting the writing time to 30–60 minutes is common in most related studies. Furthermore, the

results of a previous study revealed that given a similar task a sufficient number of Japanese EFL students could complete the whole writing procedure including post-writing activities such as revision under the 30-minute time limit (Sasaki & Hirose, 1996). In the present study, the time limit was not strictly enforced but instead was extended until they felt they had finished. See Tables 11 and 18 for the time range the participants actually spent on the tasks.

[10] Because the participants came to the data collection session without knowing they were going to write L1/L2 compositions, it was expected that not all participants had English dictionaries with them. Anticipating probable effects of a dictionary on some users' English writing, it was felt necessary to provide all participants with the same writing conditions (i.e., no dictionary use).

[11] Thus, the L1 and L2 total full scores were different. The L1 and L2 organization scores were also different, 30 and 40, respectively. Except for Tables 3 and 4, the mean percentage scores (%) were reported in this paper for the sake of simplicity.

[12] To analyze macro-level structures of student text, Kobayashi (1984) focused her analysis on the ordering of the general statement and specifics. Kubota (1992) expanded the analysis to include macro-level rhetorical patterns such as Explanation, Specification, and Induction.

[13] For macro-level rhetorical patterns, Kubota (1992) included the following five categories: Collection, Comparison, Explanation, Specification, and Induction. In the present study, I limited my categories to Explanation, Specification, and Induction because all participants stated their opinions on the topic and I found no cases of Collection ("a pattern that enumerates or lists elements") or Comparison ("a pattern that contains two elements arranged in a relation of compare/contrast, adversative or alternative") (Kubota, 1992, p. 69) in the present data.

[14] According to this view, the writer is unlikely to use a deductive pattern if the reader has stronger power/status and the writer anticipates the reader's displeasure. On the other hand, the writer can afford to employ a deductive pattern if no harm can be expected to result for being straightforward (A. Kirkpatrick, personal communication, July 1, 2003).

[15] The mean L1 total score of the deductive group (%) was 69.6, whereas that of the inductive group was 73.1.

[16] As mentioned, all the raters scored the compositions individually. Relatively low interrater reliability for L1 compositions might have been partly due to not having a norming or training session for the raters. Such a session would have been necessary to achieve a higher interrater reliability.

[17] Just as the L1 and L2 total possible scores were different, the L1 and L2

organization scores were also different. For the sake of simplicity, the mean percentage scores (%) were used to compare these scores.

[18] Translating L1 compositions into L2 may pose a question of equivalence between the two versions in terms of language use and vocabulary. L1 compositions written by less proficient student writers have mistakes in the use of language use and vocabulary. On the other hand, organization can be kept constant.

Chapter 2

[1] This chapter is an expanded version of Hirose (2002).

[2] The participants' L2 writing background was asked about in the interviews. Their L2 writing experience before they entered university had not gone beyond translation at a sentence level.

[3] With regard to the composition length, it was possible to compare L2 compositions and L2 translations of L1 compositions by the number of words. However, this may pose a compatibility problem between the two versions.

[4] Co-occurrences of **E** (rereading) with other categories such as **P**$_L$ and **L**$_L$ were also found in Anzai and Uchida (1981). Although such co-occurrences may require full discussion, it is beyond the scope of this study and thus left for further investigation.

[5] This is not a complete list of categories used in Anzai and Uchida (1981). Only those coded in the protocol data of the low-proficiency group were listed in Table 13.

[6] In the present study, the recall protocol data was collected in L1 after they finished writing. The participants reported what they wanted to write in Japanese. It was difficult to judge whether while pausing they were translating or attempting to put their thoughts into words. The development of a better method during L2 writing appears to be necessary to scrutinize L1 use.

Chapter 3

[1] This chapter is an expanded version of Hirose (2003a).

[2] According to Jacobs et al. (1981), the word range between 200 and 300 is desirable for ESL compositions written in 30 minutes. The high students in the present study, not to mention low students, did not achieve this word level except Ichiro. Although it may not be fair to apply the ESL standards to EFL students' writing performances, there is no accepted standard of EFL word ranges. Until such EFL word ranges have been established, referring to Jacobs et al.'s (1981) word level should be permissible.

[3] It can be argued that opinion letters do not necessarily require an introductory paragraph or a conclusion paragraph. Nevertheless, it was noticeable that the

students in the present study all wrote an introductory paragraph but did not necessarily form a concluding paragraph in L2. Those who did not produce a concluding paragraph either made a concluding statement at the sentence level in the final paragraph or chose not to make such a statement because the writing was meant to be an opinion letter.

4 In a larger confirmatory study, the topics need to be alternated in the two languages to control for topic effects.

Chapter 4

1 This chapter is a revised English version of Hirose (2003b).

2 The two proficiency groups of Kobayashi and Rinnert (1992) roughly corresponded to those of the present study in terms of their L2 proficiency levels. The high and low groups in Kobayashi and Rinnert (1992) had mean scores of 78.9 and 66 for structure section of CELT, respectively. The high and low groups in the present study had mean scores of 88.7 and 54.8, respectively (recall Table 1).

Chapter 5

1 This chapter is an extensively revised version of Hirose (1998).

2 The ranges of student variables such as age, L2 learning background, L2 proficiency and writing ability levels were wide.

3 Although the participants took the writing course for the first time at the university, the good writers, as opposed to the weak writers, had previous self-initiated writing experiences in L2 and did not consider L2 writing difficult. Probably it is the weak writer group who would better represent Japanese university students taking the first L2 writing course.

4 The introductory section of the chapter on "Personal Opinion" goes as follows:

> The purpose of personal opinion paragraphs is to express the writer's opinion. However, in the paragraph, the writer must do more than just express an opinion. The writer must also give support for the opinion, that is, reasons for holding that opinion.
>
> One way of writing a personal opinion paragraph is to state the opinion in the introduction. Then, in the discussion, the writer gives facts, arguments or supportive data for that opinion. In the conclusion, the writer restates the opinion or summarizes the arguments or facts. Another way of writing a personal opinion paragraph is to mention the opinions of one or more other people or groups and then agree or disagree with the opinions in the introduction. Again, in the discussion, the writer gives support for his or her opinion and in the conclusion

restates the opinion or summarizes the supporting data. (Kitao & Kitao, 1988, p. 37)

[5] After their comparisons, each of them was provided a copy of the scores (filled-out ESL Composition Profile forms) for the two compositions.

[6] In his analysis, the writer reported that although the topic sentence was placed at the beginning in both compositions, the topic sentence was grammatically unclear in the pre-composition, whereas the topic sentence in the post-composition was clearly stated.

Chapter 6

[1] This chapter is an extensively revised English version of Hirose (1997).

[2] The participants in Chapter 6 were day school students, whereas those in Chapter 5 were night school students. This is one of the reasons the participants in Chapter 6 had higher, and narrower range of, L2 proficiency levels than those in Chapter 5, despite the fact that they both took a course whose title was the same.

[3] The pre- and post-composition tasks used in the present chapter were different from those used in the previous chapter in several ways. First, different topics were chosen, as opposed to the same topic used in Chapter 5, because this could avoid possible influences of participants' thinking about the topic over time. Second, the prompt used in Chapter 5 was revised to include descriptions of the intended reader and purpose of writing for Chapter 6. Third, the writing time was extended to 30 minutes in the present chapter. As discussed in the previous chapter, a substantial number of participants reported that they felt a 20-minute writing time short for completing especially in the post-composition.

References

Achiba, M., & Kuromiya, Y. (1983). Rhetorical patterns extant in the English compositions of Japanese students. *JALT Journal, 5*, 1-13.

Anzai, Y., & Uchida, N. (1981). Kodomo wa ikani sakubun o kakuka? [How do children produce writings?] *Japanese Journal of Educational Psychology, 29*, 323-332.

Arndt, V. (1987). Six writers in search of texts: A protocol-based study of L1 and L2 writing. *ELT Journal, 41*, 257-267.

Bereiter, C., & Scardamalia, M. (1987). *The psychology of written composition*. Hillsdale, NJ: Lawrence Erlbaum.

Bosher, S. (1998). The composing process of three Southeast Asian writers at the post-secondary levels: An exploratory study. *Journal of Second Language Writing, 7*, 205-241.

Carter, M. (1990). The idea of expertise: An exploration of cognitive and social dimensions of writing. *College Composition and Communication, 41*, 265-286.

Casanave, C. P. (1994). Language development in students' journals. *Journal of Second Language Writing, 3*, 179-201.

―――. (1998). Transitions: The balancing act of bilingual academics. *Journal of Second Language Writing, 7*, 205-241.

Cohen, A. (1990). *Language learning: Insights for learners, teachers, and researchers*. New York: Newbury House.

Connor, U. (1996). *Contrastive rhetoric: Cross-cultural aspects of second-language writing*. New York: Cambridge University Press.

Cumming, A. (1989). Writing expertise and second language proficiency. *Language Learning, 39*, 81-141.

―――. (1990). Metalinguistic and ideational thinking in second language composing. *Written Communication, 7*, 482-511.

de Larios, J.R., Murphy, L., & Manchon, R. (1999). The use of restructuring strategies in EFL writing: A study of Spanish learners of English as a foreign language. *Journal of Second Language Writing, 8*, 13-44.

Flower, L.S., & Hayes, J.R. (1981). A cognitive process of writing. *College Composition and Communication, 32*, 365-387.

Friedlander, A. (1990). Composing in English: Effects of a first language on writing in English as s second language. In B. Kroll (Ed.), *Second language writing: Research insights for the classroom* (pp. 109-125). Cambridge: Cambridge University Press.

Fukushima, S. (1985). Teaching English composition by putting emphasis on the paragraph. In K. Kitao (Ed.), *TEFL in Japan: JALT 10th anniversary collected papers* (pp. 193-201). Kyoto: JALT.

Fukushima, S., & Sato, T. (1989). The effectiveness of teaching transition words in EFL composition class. *Kantô Kôsinetsu Eigo Kyôiku Gakkai Kenkyû Kiyô*, 3, 29-39.

Goldstein, L.M. (1993). Becoming a member of the "teaching foreign languages" community: Integrating reading and writing through an adjunct/content course. In J.G. Carson & I. Leki (Eds.), *Reading in the composition classroom: Second language perspectives* (pp. 290-298). Boston: Heinle & Heinle.

Gosden, H. (1996). Verbal reports of Japanese novices' research writing practices in English. *Journal of Second Language Writing*, 5, 109-128.

Greene, S., & Higgins, L. (1994). "Once upon a time": The use of retrospective accounts in building theory in composition. In P. Smagorinsky (Ed.), *Speaking about writing: Reflections on research methodology* (pp. 115-140). Thousand Oaks, CA: Sage.

Hale, G. (1992). *Effects of amount of time allowed on the test of written English*. Princeton, NJ: Educational Testing Service.

Hall, C. (1990). Managing the complexity of revising across languages. *TESOL Quarterly*, 24, 43-60.

Hamp-Lyons, L. (1990). Second language writing: Assessment issues. In B. Kroll (Ed.), *Second language writing: Research insights for the classroom* (pp. 69-87). New York: Cambridge University Press.

Harris, D. P., & Palmer, L. A. (1986). *CELT: Examiners' instructions and technical manual*. New York: McGraw-Hill.

Hashiuchi, T. (1995). *Paragurafu raitingu nyûmon* [An introduction to paragraph writing]. Tokyo: Kenkyusha.

Hayes, J.R. (1996). A new framework for understanding cognition and affect in writing. In C.M. Levy & S. Ransdell (Eds.), *The science of writing* (pp. 1-27). Mahwah, NJ: Lawrence Erlbaum Associates.

Hayes, J.R., & Flower, L.S. (1980). Identifying the organization of writing processes. In L.W. Gregg & E.R. Steinberg (Eds.), *Cognitive processes in writing* (pp. 3-30). Mahwah, NJ: Lawrence Erlbaum Associates.

Henry, A.R. (1993). *Second language rhetorics in process: A comparison of Arabic, Chinese, and Spanish*. New York: Peter Lang.

Hinds, J. (1983). Contrastive rhetoric: Japanese and English. *Text*, 3, 183-196.

———. (1987). Reader vs. writer responsibility: A new typology. In U. Connor & R. Kaplan (Eds.), *Writing across languages: Analysis of L2 text* (pp. 141-152).

Reading, MA: Addison-Wesley.

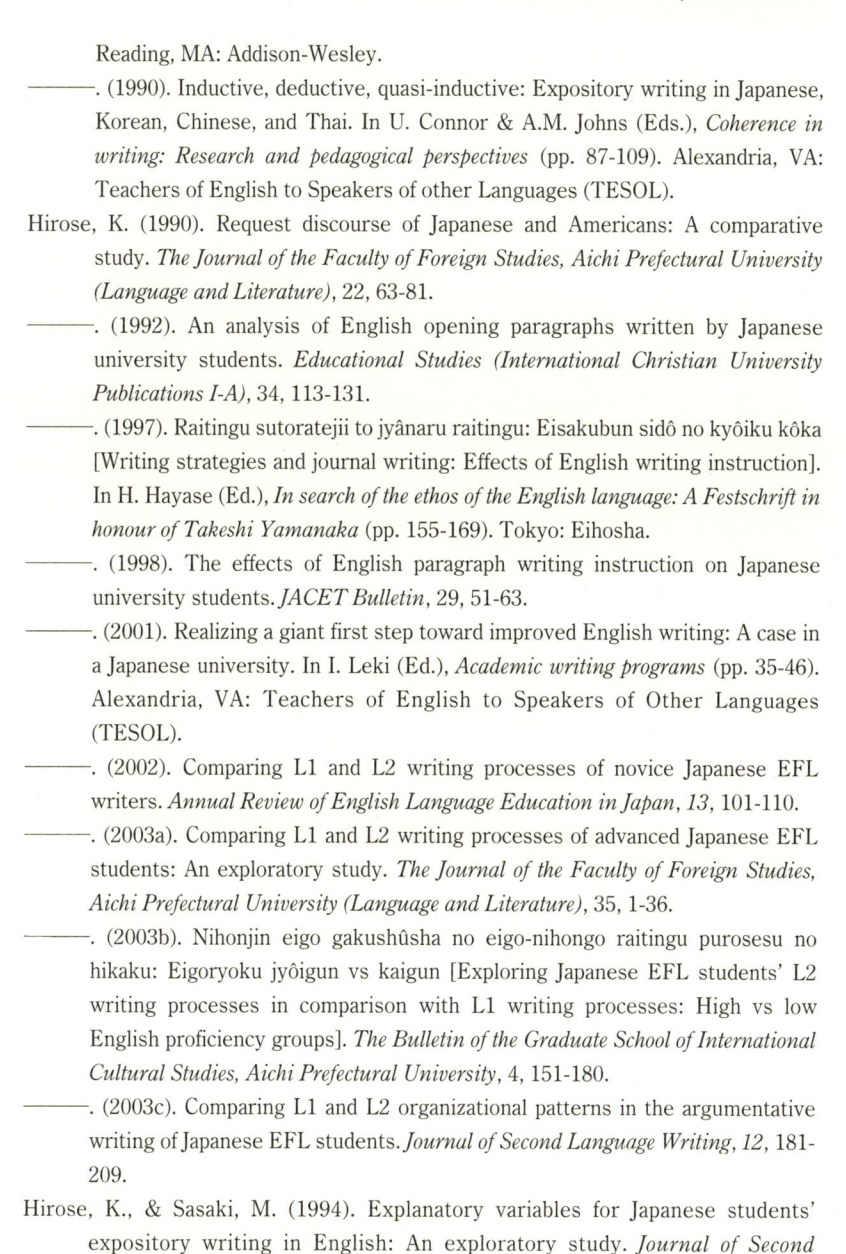

———. (1990). Inductive, deductive, quasi-inductive: Expository writing in Japanese, Korean, Chinese, and Thai. In U. Connor & A.M. Johns (Eds.), *Coherence in writing: Research and pedagogical perspectives* (pp. 87-109). Alexandria, VA: Teachers of English to Speakers of other Languages (TESOL).

Hirose, K. (1990). Request discourse of Japanese and Americans: A comparative study. *The Journal of the Faculty of Foreign Studies, Aichi Prefectural University (Language and Literature)*, 22, 63-81.

———. (1992). An analysis of English opening paragraphs written by Japanese university students. *Educational Studies (International Christian University Publications I-A)*, 34, 113-131.

———. (1997). Raitingu sutoratejii to jyânaru raitingu: Eisakubun sidô no kyôiku kôka [Writing strategies and journal writing: Effects of English writing instruction]. In H. Hayase (Ed.), *In search of the ethos of the English language: A Festschrift in honour of Takeshi Yamanaka* (pp. 155-169). Tokyo: Eihosha.

———. (1998). The effects of English paragraph writing instruction on Japanese university students. *JACET Bulletin*, 29, 51-63.

———. (2001). Realizing a giant first step toward improved English writing: A case in a Japanese university. In I. Leki (Ed.), *Academic writing programs* (pp. 35-46). Alexandria, VA: Teachers of English to Speakers of Other Languages (TESOL).

———. (2002). Comparing L1 and L2 writing processes of novice Japanese EFL writers. *Annual Review of English Language Education in Japan*, 13, 101-110.

———. (2003a). Comparing L1 and L2 writing processes of advanced Japanese EFL students: An exploratory study. *The Journal of the Faculty of Foreign Studies, Aichi Prefectural University (Language and Literature)*, 35, 1-36.

———. (2003b). Nihonjin eigo gakushûsha no eigo-nihongo raitingu purosesu no hikaku: Eigoryoku jyôigun vs kaigun [Exploring Japanese EFL students' L2 writing processes in comparison with L1 writing processes: High vs low English proficiency groups]. *The Bulletin of the Graduate School of International Cultural Studies, Aichi Prefectural University*, 4, 151-180.

———. (2003c). Comparing L1 and L2 organizational patterns in the argumentative writing of Japanese EFL students. *Journal of Second Language Writing*, 12, 181-209.

Hirose, K., & Sasaki, M. (1994). Explanatory variables for Japanese students' expository writing in English: An exploratory study. *Journal of Second Language Writing*, 3, 203-229.

Hirose, K., & Sasaki, M. (2000). Effects of teaching metaknowledge and journal writing on Japanese university students' EFL writing. *JALT Journal, 22*, 94-113.

Horowitz, D. M. (1986). Process, not product: Less than meets the eye. *TESOL Quarterly, 20*, 141-144.

Hughey, J. B., Wormuth, D.R., Hartfiel, V.F., & Jacobs, H.L. (1983). *Teaching ESL composition*. Rowley, MA: Newbury House.

Igarashi, J., Inada, K., Iwamura, S., Fujimoto, R. & Yuasa, N. (1976). Daigaku eigo kyôiku ni kansuru ankêto chôsa—Hiroshima daigaku ni okeru gakusei no iken [A questionnaire survey on college English education: Students' opinions at Hiroshima University]. *Notes on Higher Education* (Research Institute for Higher Education, Hiroshima University), no. 20.

JACET Kansai Chapter Writing Teaching Group (Eds.) (1995). *Daigaku ni okeru eisakubun sidô no arikata: Eisakubun jittai chôsa no hôkoku* [English writing instruction at the university levels in Japan: A survey of English writing instruction]. Kyoto: Authors.

Jacobs, H.L., Zinkgraf, S.A., Wormuth, D.R., Hartfiel, V.F., & Hughey, J.B. (1981). *Testing ESL composition: A practical approach*. Rowley, MA: Newbury House.

Jones, S., & Tetroe, J. (1987). Composing in a second language. In A. Matsuhashi (Ed.), *Writing in real time: Modeling production processes* (pp. 34-57). Norwood, NJ: Ablex.

Kabashima, T., Uegaki, S., Soda, F., & Satake, H. (1989). *Fukutake kokugo jiten* [Fukutake Japanese dictionary]. Tokyo: Fukutake Shoten.

Kamimura, T. (1996). Composing in Japanese as a first language and English as a foreign language: A study of narrative writing. *RELC Journal, 27*, 47-69.

Kaplan, R. B. (1966). Cultural thought patterns in intercultural education. *Language Learning, 16*, 1-20.

Kawaijuku Shôronbunka (Department of Shôronbun, Kawaijuku) (2002). *2002 nendo daigaku nyûsi shôronbun mondaishû* [Collections of shôronbun for university entrance examinations in the year 2002]. Tokyo: Kawai Shuppan.

Kinoshita, K. (1981). *Rikakei no sakubun gijyutsu* [Writing skills for scientific writing]. Tokyo: Chuo Koronsha.

———. (1990). *Repôto no kumitate kata* [How to organize papers]. Tokyo: Chikuma Shobo.

Kirkpatrick, A. (1997). Traditional Chinese text structures and their influence on the writing in Chinese and English of contemporary mainland Chinese students. *Journal of Second Language Writing, 6*, 223-244.

Kitao, S. K., & Kitao, K. (1988). *Writing English paragraphs.* Tokyo: Eichosha Shinsha.

Kobayashi, H. (1984). *Rhetorical patterns in English and Japanese.* Unpublished doctoral dissertation, Teachers College, Columbia University.

Kobayashi, H., & Rinnert, C. (1992). Effects of first language on second language writing: Translation versus direct composition. *Language Learning, 42,* 183-215.

———. (1996). Factors affecting composition evaluation in an EFL context: Cultural rhetorical pattern and readers' background. *Language Learning, 46,* 397-437.

———. (2002). High school student perceptions of first language literacy instruction: Implications for second language writing. *Journal of Second Language Writing, 11,* 91-116.

Koike, I., Ando, S., Furukawa, S., Haraoka, S., Ibe, S., Ito, K., Ishida, M., Kuniyoshi, T., Masukawa, K., Nishimura, Y., Tada, M., & Tanabe, Y. (1983). *Daigaku eigo kyôiku ni kansuru jittai to shôraizo no sôgôteki kenkyû (I)—Kyôin no tachiba* [General survey of English language teaching at colleges and universities in Japan (I): Teachers' view]. Tokyo: Research Group for University English Teaching in Japan.

Koike, I., Ando, S., Furukawa, S., Haraoka, S., Ibe, S., Ito, K., Ishida, M., Ishikawa, S., Kuniyoshi, T., Matsuyama, M., Narisawa, Y., Nishimura, Y., Tada, M., Tajima, K., Tanabe, Y., & Yoshioka, M. (1985). *Daigaku eigo kyôiku ni kansuru jittai to shôraizo no sôgôteki kenkyû (II)—Gakusei no tachiba* [General survey of English language teaching at colleges and universities in Japan (II): Students' view]. Tokyo: Research Group for University English Teaching in Japan.

Krapels, A.R. (1990). An overview of second language writing process research. In B. Kroll (Ed.), *Second language writing: Research insights for the classroom* (pp. 37-56). Cambridge: Cambridge University Press.

Kresovich, B.M. (1988). The journal assignment in composition class at a Japanese university. *Bulletin of the College of Education, University of the Ryukyus, 33,* 71-83.

Kubota, R. (1992). *Contrastive rhetoric of Japanese and English: A critical approach.* Unpublished doctoral dissertation. University of Toronto.

———. (1998a). An investigation of Japanese and English L1 essay organization: Differences and similarities. *The Canadian Modern Language Review, 54,* 475-507.

———. (1998b). An investigation of L1-L2 transfer in writing among Japanese university students: Implications for contrastive rhetoric. *Journal of Second Language Writing, 7,* 69-100.

Leggett, A. (1966). Notes on the writing of scientific English for Japanese physicists. *Butsuri (Nihon Butsuri Gakkaisi), 21*, 790-805.

———. (1975). Notes on the writing of scientific English for Japanese physicists. In Nihon Butsuri Gakkai [the Physical Society of Japan] (Eds.), *Jyânaru no ronbun o yokusuru tameni: Butsurigaku ronbun no chosha eno michi* [Improving papers for journals: Ways to publish papers for writers in physics] (Expanded Version) (pp. 96-110). Tokyo: Nihon Butsuri Gakkai. (Original work published in 1966)

———. (1984). Notes on the writing of scientific English for Japanese physicists (S. Hirano, Trans.). In Nihon Butsuri Gakkai [the Physical Society of Japan] (Eds.), *Kagaku eigoronbun no subete* [All about scientific English papers] (pp. 165-195). Tokyo: Maruzen.

Leki, I. (1990). Coaching from the margins: Issues in written response. In B. Kroll (Ed.), *Second language writing: Research insights for the classroom* (pp. 57-68). Cambridge: Cambridge University Press.

———. (1992). *Understanding ESL writers: A guide for teachers*. Portsmouth, NH: Boynton/Cook.

Liebman, J. (1992). Toward a new contrastive rhetoric: Differences between Arabic and Japanese rhetorical instruction. *Journal of Second Language Writing, 1*, 141-165.

Littlejohn, A. (1991). *Writing 2*. Cambridge: Cambridge University Press.

———. (1994). *Writing 4*. Cambridge: Cambridge University Press.

Livingston, S. (1987, April). *The effects of time limits on the quality of student-written essays*. Paper presented at the meeting of the American Educational Research Association, Washington, DC.

Loveday, L. (1983). Rhetoric patterns in conflict: The sociocultural relativity of discourse-organizing processes. *Journal of Pragmatics, 7*, 169-190.

Matsuda, P.K. (1997). Contrastive rhetoric in context: A dynamic model of L2 writing. *Journal of Second Language Writing, 6*, 45-60.

Maynard, S.K. (1996). Presentation of one's view in Japanese newspaper columns: Commentary strategies and sequencing. *Text, 16*, 391-421.

McCagg, P. (1996). If you can lead a horse to water, you don't have to make it drink: Some comments on reader and writer responsibilities. *Multilingua, 15*, 239-256.

McCornick, A. (1993). Journal writing and the damaged language learner. In C. P. Casanave (Ed.), *Journal writing: Pedagogical perspectives* (pp. 6-17). Institute of Language and Communication, Keio University, SFC (Shonan Fujisawa Campus).

McDonough, S. (1995). *Strategy and skill in learning a foreign language*. London: Edward Arnold.

Miyata, O. (1994). Paragraph writing no gakushû wa nihonbun no ronrisei o takameruka [Will learning skills of good paragraph writing in English help to improve paragraph development in Japanese?] *The JACET 33rd Annual Convention Outlines* (pp. 194-197). Tokyo: JACET.

Mohan, B.A., & Lo, W. A-Y. (1985). Academic writing and Chinese students: Transfer and developmental factors. *TESOL Quarterly, 19*, 515-534.

Momoi, H. (2001). Raitingu no purosesu [Writing process]. In T. Komuro (Ed.), *Eigo raitingu ron* [Theories of English writing] (pp. 30-37). Tokyo: Kagensha.

Murai, M. (1990). Sakubun sidô no riron [Theories of composition instructions]. In K. Ôtsuki (Ed.), *Kokugokyôikugaku* [Japanese language pedagogy] (pp. 145-152). Tokyo: Fukumura Shuppan.

Naotsuka, R. (1980). *Ôbeijin ga chinmoku suru toki: Ibunka kan komyunikeishon* [When Europeans and Americans keep silent: Intercultural communication]. Tokyo: Taishukan Shoten.

Naotsuka, R., & Sakamoto, N. et al. (1981). *Mutual understanding of different cultures*. Tokyo: Taishukan Shoten.

Nihon Butsuri Gakkai [the Physical Society of Japan] (Eds.), (1975). *Jyânaru no ronbun o yokusuru tameni: Butsurigaku ronbun no chosha eno michi* [Improving papers for journals: Ways to publish papers for writers in physics] (Expanded Version). Tokyo: Nihon Butsuri Gakkai.

———. (Eds.), (1984). *Kagaku eigoronbun no subete* [All about scientific English papers]. Tokyo: Maruzen.

Nishigaki, C., & Leishman, S. (1998). Some effects of classroom instruction developed from students' needs analysis: Composition at the university level. *Bulletin of the Faculty of Education*, Chiba University, *46*, 61-69.

Oi, K. (1984). *Cross-cultural differences in rhetorical patterning: A study of Japanese and English*. Unpublished doctoral dissertation. State University of New York at Stony Brook.

———. (1986). Cross-cultural differences in rhetorical patterning: A study of Japanese and English. *JACET Bulletin*, 17, 23-48.

Okabe, R. (1983). Cultural assumptions of East and West: Japan and the United States. In W. Gudykunst (Ed.), *Intercultural communication theory: Current perspectives* (pp. 21-44). Newbury Park: Sage.

Ôkuma, T. (1997). Kokusaika jidai jyôhôka jidai niokeru ronritekina bunshô o kakukoto no igi [The significance of writing logical sentences in the eras of internationalization and information]. In Chugakkô Kokugoka Kyôiku Jissen Kôza Kankôkai (Eds.), *Chugakkô kokugoka kyôiku jissen kôza dai 4 kan* [Practical seminar in Japanese language education at junior high school Vol. 4] (pp. 218-221). Tokyo: Nichibun.

Ôoka, M. et al. (1998). *Kokugo hyôgen* [Japanese writing]. Tokyo: Shougaku Tosho.

Pennington, M.C., Costa, V., So, S., Shing, J.L.W., Hirose, K., & Niedzielski, K. (1997). The teaching of English-as-a-second-language writing in the Asia-Pacific region: A cross-country comparison. *RELC Journal, 28*, 120-143.

Pennington, M.C., & So, S. (1993). Comparing writing process and product across two languages: A study of 6 Singaporean university student writers. *Journal of Second Language Writing, 2*, 41-63.

Pianko, S. (1979). A description of the composing processes of college freshman writers. *Research in the Teaching of English, 13*, 5-22.

Raimes, A. (1985). What unskilled ESL students do as they write: A classroom study of composing. *TESOL Quarterly, 19*, 229-259.

———. (1987). Language proficiency, writing ability, and composing strategies: A study of ESL college student writers. *Language Learning, 37*, 439-468.

Ramanathan, V., & Atkinson, D. (1999). Individualism, academic writing, and ESL writers. *Journal of Second Language Writing, 8*, 45-75.

Reid, J. (1984). The radical outliner and the radical brainstormer: A perspective on composing processes. *TESOL Quarterly, 18*, 529-534.

———. (1990). Responding to different topic types: A quantitative analysis from a contrastive rhetoric perspective. In B. Kroll (Ed.), *Second language writing: Research insights for the classroom* (pp. 191-210). Cambridge: Cambridge University Press.

Rinnert, C., & Kobayashi, H. (2001). Differing perceptions of EFL writing among readers in Japan. *Modern Language Journal, 85*, 189-209.

Ross, S., Shortreed, I. M., & Robb, T. N. (1988). First language composition pedagogy in the second language classroom. *RELC Journal, 19*, 29-48.

Sasaki, M. (2000). Toward an empirical model of EFL writing processes: An exploratory study. *Journal of Second Language Writing, 9*, 259-291.

Sasaki, M., & Hirose, K. (1996). Explanatory variables for EFL students' expository writing. *Language Learning, 46*, 137-174.

———. (1999). Development of an analytic rating scale for Japanese L1 writing. *Language Testing, 16*, 457-478.

Scardamalia, M., Bereiter, C., & Steinbach, R. (1984). Teachability of reflective processes in written composition. *Cognitive Science, 8*, 173-190.

Silva, T. (1990). Second language composition instruction: Developments, issues, and directions in ESL. In B. Kroll (Ed.), *Second language writing: Research insights for the classroom* (pp. 11-23). Cambridge: Cambridge University Press.

———. (1992). L1 vs L2 writing: ESL graduate students' perceptions. *TESL Canada Journal/Revue TESL du Canada, 10*, 27-47.

———. (1993). Toward an understanding of the distinct nature of L2 writing: The ESL research and its implications. *TESOL Quarterly, 27*, 657-677.

Smagorinsky, P. (1991). The writer's knowledge and the writing process: A protocol analysis. *Research in the Teaching of English, 25*, 339-364.

Sugimoto, T. (1989). Bunshô o kaku katei [Cognitive processes of writing]. In *Kyôka rikai no ninchi sinrigaku* [Cognitive psychology of understanding school subjects] (pp. 1-48). Tokyo: Shin'yousha.

Susser, B. (1994). Process approaches in ESL/EFL writing instruction. *Journal of Second Language Writing, 3*, 31-47.

Suzuki, H. (1993). Kokusai densi mêru riyô no eisakubun sidô roku nenkan no sôkatu [A review of six years of using e-mail in English writing instruction]. *The Proceedings of the Department of Foreign Languages and Literature, College of Arts and Sciences, The University of Tokyo, 41*, 12-33.

Tabachnick, B.G., & Fidell, L.S. (1996). *Using multivariate statistics* (3rd ed.). New York: Harper Collins College Publishers.

Uchida, N. (1989). Kodomo no suikô hôryaku no hattatsu: sakubun niokeru jikonai taiwa no katei [Development of strategies used by children in rewriting compositions: Dialectical processes in writing]. *Ochanomizu University Studies in Arts and Culture, 42*, 75-104.

———. (1990). *Kodomo no bunshô: Kakukoto kangaerukoto* [Children's compositions: Writing, thinking]. Tokyo: The University of Tokyo Press.

Uzawa, K. (1996). Second language learners' process of L1 writing, L2 writing, and translation from L1 into L2. *Journal of Second Language Writing, 5*, 271-294.

Uzawa, K., & Cumming, A. (1989). Writing strategies in Japanese as a foreign language: Lowering or keeping up the standards. *Canadian Modern Language Review, 46*, 178-194.

Wang, W., & Wen, Q. (2002). L1 use in the L2 composing process: An exploratory study of 16 Chinese EFL writers. *Journal of Second Language Writing, 11*, 225-246.

Zamel, V. (1983). The composing processes of advanced ESL students: Six case studies. *TESOL Quarterly, 17*, 165-187.

Appendixes

Appendix A: Macro-Level Organizational Patterns*

1. <u>Explanation (Collection)</u>: The writer's opinion on the topic is presented and then supporting reasons are enumerated.
    <u>Explanation (Comparison)</u>: The writer's opinion on the topic is presented and then a supporting reason is presented by comparing or contrasting two elements.
2. <u>Specification (Collection)</u>: The writer's opinion *and* a preview statement of supporting reasons or a point of view for the subsequent arguments are presented, and then the reasons or arguments are explained in more detail by enumeration.
    <u>Specification (Comparison)</u>: The writer's opinion *and* a preview statement of supporting reasons or a point of view for the subsequent arguments are presented, and then the reasons or arguments are explained in more detail by comparing/contrasting two elements.
3. <u>Induction</u>: The main idea is placed at the end and preceding arguments constitute supporting reason(s) for it.
    <u>Induction (Collection)</u>: The writer's opinion is realized in the final section; the preceding arguments constitute premises or reasons which are arranged in a form of enumeration.
4. <u>Other</u>: None of the above.

*This is not a complete list from Kubota (1992, pp. 70-71). Only those patterns rated in this study are listed here.

Appendix B: L1 and L2 Compositions Written by Ichiro (H)

L1:

　僕は、クリスチャンでもないのに日本人がクリスマスにパーティーを開いたり贈り物をすることについては中立的な意見を持っていますが、どちらかの立場をとるとしたら、「この習慣は、止めるべきである」と思います。というのは、そもそも日本人はクリスマスの本来の意味を取り違えているという事実があるからです。

　まず、キリスト教の国アメリカについてです。クリスマスというのは、彼らクリスチャンにとって一年の内で最も聖なる休日であり、この日は家族みんなで自宅にて、ゆっくりと食事をして会話を楽しみ、時間を共有する日なのです。一昨年のクリスマスを過ごしたカナダでも同じで、食事を一緒にさせて頂いた家庭では、まるで時間が止まってしまったかのような感覚を今でも憶えています。

　一方、日本ではクリスマスというのは、数々のイベント、デパートのセールス合戦、パーティーと題した暴飲暴食の絶好の機会。日本は仏教国で、正月というのがキリスト教でいうクリスマスなのですが、この背景には、欧米文化を模倣する傾向にある日本の特異性が見え隠れしているように思います。

　結論として、クリスマスに関する今の日本の習慣には「反対」です。が、しかしどうでしょう、クリスマスという呼び方自体を変えてみては…。クリスチャンでない以上、12月25日をクリスマスと呼ぶ必要はないでしょう。クリスマスは特に若い人々にとって今や重要な日なので、「若者の日」なんていうのはいかがでしょうか。

L1 (my translation of original Japanese):

　　　I have a neutral opinion about the issue that Japanese, although they are not Christians, hold parties or exchange presents at Christmas. If I take either of the positions, however, I think that "this custom should be abolished." This is because it is the fact that Japanese misunderstand the real meaning of Christmas.

　　　First, a case of a Christian country, the United States. Christmas is for Christians the most holy holiday in a year, and it is the day when all family members share their time having leisurely dinner and enjoying conversations together. Canada, where I spent Christmas the year before, is the same. I still remember the sense I had when I dined with a family as if the time had stopped.

On the other hand, in Japan, Christmas provides an opportunity for various events, sales competitions between department stores, eating and drinking times with the name of a party. Japan is a Buddhist country and the New Year's Day is the counterpart of Christmas for Christianity. I think Japanese celebrating Christmas shows their peculiarity prone to imitate European and American culture in the background.

In conclusion, I am against the present Japanese custom concerning Christmas. But how about this idea, change the name of Christmas? Japanese do not have to call December 25th Christmas because they are not Christians. Christmas is now an important day especially for young Japanese, so why don't we call the day "Youth Day" instead?

L2:

I know a school uniform is a kind of strange to those who are living out of Japan. When I was in a college in the U. S., I read an article that was about a school uniform in Japan. I was an only foreigner in that class, and almost every classmate looked surprised at the fact that there's a school uniform in Japanese schools. Regardless, I still thought a school uniform in Japan is okay.

One of the main reasons why I'm for a school uniform is that I'm worried about the Japanese characteristic that everyone wants to look better than others. Parents want their kids look better than kids in neiborhood, and kids also try to make themselves look better than others. As a result, kids' clothing could be much expensive and too good if there's no school uniform.

I also think a school uniform would help kids dress well without clothing. They would arrange their hair cut, they could have nice pairs of shoes, and they might choose good-looking bags by themselves.

Another reason why I stand for a school uniform is that I don't want kids dress as they like because I had to have a school uniform. School regulation forced me to wear a school uniform. What is strange is that nobody complained. We regard a school uniform as a kind of Japanese culture.

Note: Spelling, grammar, and word choice are left intact.

Appendix C: L1 and L2 Compositions Written by Hikari (H)

L1:

　日本は、明治以降盛んに外国（特に欧米）の文化や習慣を取り入れてきた。クリスマスは、今では日本独自の習慣として生まれたものであるかのように自然なものとして捉えられている。とは言え、日本でのクリスマスは、クリスチャンのクリスマスが持つ宗教的意義をほとんど意識しておらず、パーティーや贈り物をするためのきっかけの一つにすぎない。

　クリスマスは、子供からお年寄りまで、誰にでも楽しめる一日である。子供は、クリスマス・イヴにサンタクロースがそっと枕元に置いてゆくプレゼントを心待ちにし、若者は恋人あるいは友人同士で食事に出かけたり、パーティーを開いたり、贈り物を交換したりし、親である大人は子供の喜ぶ顔を見たい一心でプレゼントを買い求め、いつもと少し違う夕食を用意する。孫を持つお年寄りも同様である。この日は、誰もが誰かの笑顔や温かみに触れたくなり、そのために自然と行動が取れるという、特別な日なのだ。

　このように、皆が幸せな優しい気持ちになれる一日、既に日本人の心に深く根づいている一日を、良い習慣と呼ばない理由は一体どこにあるのだろうか。

L1 (my translation of original Japanese):

　　　　Japan has vigorously absorbed foreign, especially European and American, culture and customs since the Meiji Era. Christmas is now considered to be taken into granted as if celebrating Christmas was an established unique Japanese custom. However, Japanese are scarcely conscious of the religious significance Christians attach to Christmas, and Christmas is just a good chance for them to hold parties or give presents.

　　　　Christmas is a day when anyone, from a kid to an elderly person, can enjoy themselves. Children look forward to presents that Santa Claus gently puts down near their pillows on Christmas Eve. Young people go out for dinner, hold a party, or exchange presents with friends or lovers. Adults who are parents buy presents for their children only to see them delighted with their presents, and prepare dinner slightly different from their usual meal. The elderly people who have grandchildren do the same. This day is a special day in the sense that anyone wants to see someone's smile or feel his/her warmth, and for this purpose they can take action naturally.

Whatever reasons do we have not to call such a day when everyone feels happy and gentle, and the day that has already taken deep root in Japanese minds, a good custom?

L2:

Junior high or high school students should wear uniforms, because that helps students concentrate on studying only. They don't need to think which clothes they are going to wear every morning. They don't need to think whether they look cool or sophisticated when they go to school. They don't need to buy many clothes that cost much to them, who are not allowed to work part-time.

Students are to study hard. They are never to do part-time job behind their teachers' back to make money for fashion. Schools should offer an ideal atmosphere for students to study hard and uniforms are inevitable for that.

Note: Spelling, grammar, and word choice are left intact.

Appendix D: L1 and L2 Compositions Written by Chihiro (L)

L1:

　自分も例外ではないが、人間というものは何かイベントや行事などがあると、それが一般的に考えて良い事か悪い事かは別にして、それについて興味がわいたり、気分が向揚するものだと、自分は考えている。この観点から見てみるとクリスチャンであろうがなかろうが、クリスマスパーティーという1つのイベントは人が何らかの興味を示すのは当然のことである。それについて良い習慣であるか悪い習慣であるかということは誰にも決定できないと思う。もし決定できる人がいるとしたらその人はまったくクリスマスに興味を持たず何も知らない人であり、そのような人は存在しない。クリスマスについての習慣を止めるべきと考える人はおそらくクリスマスという意味についてのこだわりや信念があるに違いない。私の聞いた話ではクリスチャンの人はクリスマスには特別何もやらないということだった。この話を聞いて正直私は驚いた。それまではクリスチャンだからこそクリスチャン以外の人よりも盛大に何かを催すと考えていたからだ。その話を聞いた後は私もクリスマスについての意味について少し考えてみる必要があるのではないかと思った。しかしクリスマスという1つのイベントが自分にとっての喜び、楽しみ、プラスの方向に向かうきっかけとなれば、存在していても良い事ではないだろうか。

L1 (my translation of original Japanese):

　　　Although I am not an exception, I think people tend to become interested or inspired when an event or a function takes place, aside from whether it is generally a good thing or bad one. From this point of view, it is natural that an event of Christmas party should arouse people's interests, regardless of whether they are Christians or not. I think nobody can make a decision of whether it is a good custom or a bad custom. If there is a person who can make such a decision, the person must have no interest in Christmas or know nothing about it. Such a person does not exist. Those who think customs of Christmas should be abolished must probably have particular feelings and beliefs regarding the meaning of Christmas. I have heard that Christians do nothing special on Christmas Day. When I heard this, to be honest, I was surprised. Until that time I had thought Christians hold something more enthusiastically than non-Christians do. After I heard this, I thought I needed to think about the meaning of Christmas a little. But if an event of Christmas can be a good chance for one's delight, fun, and plus orientation, isn't it worth existing?

L2:

    I wore salor suit when I was junior high school or high school. I went to those school without I didn't take any loss to choose to wear things. I had better those things, because if I wore anything wears, I cost a lot of money and I took a lot of time. I think I didn't need those things. I think young person need other thinking things. And as other reason is we think about wears after we graduate from high school. Actually I think more about wears after I graduate from high school. But the other hand we may say fail to individuality. I think if students will wear variable wears, and students will enjoy more in school life and students will express more each individuality. But I think young person need any other things and I wish young person look forward to any other things.

Note: Spelling, grammar, and word choice are left intact.

Appendix E: L1 and L2 Compositions Written by Emi (L)

L1:

今まではこういうことについてまじめに考えなかった。というかどっちつかずという立場だった。が、この課題を与えられて、これを機に考えてみようと思う。

　日本という国は多種の文化が入り混じった国家である。それは今までのこの国の歴史を知れば分かるだろう。平安時代には中国のさまざまな文化が、戦国時代ごろはポルトガル、明治には西欧の文化が入ってきた。話がそれてしまったが、私は良い習慣の方に肩入れしようと思う。というのはクリスマスというのが日本の文化の中にもう入り込んでしまっているからである。それを今さら「良くない習慣だから止める」なんて言っても誰も聞き入れないだろう。それからもう一つ、お互いの国の良い文化はとり入れ合ったら良いのだと思う。野球の試合だって、審判は一人ではない。いろいろな角度から見れるようにたくさんいる。文化だって同じことではないか。一つの、その国独自の文化だけで国をまとめていこうものならその国は間違いなく孤立するし、自分たちが一番だという錯覚を起こすだろう。しかし、これは私の考えであって、一概には言えない。例えば中国やアフリカの奥地の人たちなんかは、彼らは彼らで村を形成してるし、他の文化の入りこむすきますらない。そういう所はちゃんと自分たちの文化に誇りをもっている。そういうところはおいといて、最終的にはやっぱり良い習慣だということになる。

L1 (my translation of original Japanese):

Up until now I have never thought about this kind of things seriously. Or rather, I did not take either side. Given this task, I want to take this opportunity to think about this.

　Japan is a country that has incorporated many kinds of cultures. If you get to know the history of this country, you will understand this. Various types of cultures came to Japan from China in the Heian Era, Portuguese cultures in the Sengoku Era, and Western European cultures in the Meiji Era. Although I diverge from the topic, I think I want to take the side of agreeing with the view that this is a good custom. This is because Christmas has been incorporated in the Japanese culture. Now no one will listen to the view that "we should abolish the custom because it is not a good custom."

There is another reason. I think it is good for each country to include each other's good cultures. Even baseball games have more than one umpire in order to watch a play from various angles. Isn't culture the same? If you want to stick to the country's unique cultures only, without doubt the country will be isolated and the people will be under the illusion that they are number one. But this is my own idea, and this is not necessarily true. For example, in China or in the backwoods of Africa, the people form their village in their own ways and they have no room for other cultures to enter. In such places, they are proud of their own culture. Aside from those places, finally, this is a good custom.

L2:

When I was a junior high school student, I was suprised at to hear that there is nothing school uniforms in the American school. Japan has had school uniforms since Meigi gidai. So Japanese think that to wear school uniform is natural.

Now I don't wear a school uniform, because I am a College student. So I am very hard every morning. According to effect, I think that school uniforms are good. To wear school uniforms are not only schools. In the company, worker are wearing uniforms. I am also wearing uniform in my company. I wear school uniform, and I get my spirit. But, some of them think that to wear school uniforms don't indrect their personality. The idea is not mistake. But, what will happen if there is nothing school uniforms now. I think that selfish young person incresingly. To wear school uniforms made us understand that We are in this company or society.

Note: Spelling, grammar, and word choice are left intact.

Appendix F: Notes and Compositions Written by Ginko (H)

L1:
Notes

○ 楽しい習慣.

○ 楽しむことができる.

○ もう何年も続いている. すでにとけこんでいる

○ 他の外国の習慣も同じ
　　　　　　もの
日本のもの, 習慣だけで生活していくことは
今では無理.

○ クリスチャンにとってのクリスマスとは
意味がちがうが, これは「日本のクリスマス」
で悪いことではない

○ 今. やめたからといってどうなるのか
他のこともやめるべきなのか

Composition

　この習慣をやめる必要はないと思う。まず第1に、楽しむことのできる習慣をわざわざなくさなくてもよいと思う。また、「クリスチャンでもないのに」といっても、もう何十年も続いてきた「日本の」習慣の1つとして溶けこんでいるのだから、「クリスチャン」にこだわる必要はない。他の国々でも各国のクリスマスというものがあると思うが、国民全てが「クリスチャン」である国などないに等しいと思う。クリスチャンではなくても、「クリスマス」という習慣を楽しんでいる人は世界中にもたくさんいるのではないか。

　また、現在の日本で、外国の習慣やものを排除してしまったら、生活してはいけないだろう。服装から社会の制度、食べ物にもいろんな国の要素が入ってきている。また、世界から輸入しているものも多い。それをクリスマスに限って排除しようというのは成り立たない。

　確かに日本でのクリスマスは本来のクリスマスの意味とは違っているかもしれないが、それはそれで長年続いてきたものだし、別にクリスチャンを冒とくするようなものではなく、逆に楽しみを共有できるのだからよいことなのではないか。

　たとえ今、「クリスマスをやめる」といったところで何のメリットがあるのだろうか。やめたからといって今の日本がよくなるわけではない。それなら大いに楽しんだ方が得だろう。

　Note: The underlined parts are verbatim copy from the notes, whereas the wavy underlined parts are paraphrases from the notes.

L2:
Notes

制服がある場合
　○ みんなが同じ．個性がない．
　○ きちんとしたかっこう
　○ 夏．冬　あつい．さむい．
　○ 動きにくい．

①ない場合.
　②自分の好きなかっこう. 個性.
　＊勝手なかっこう. → 個人の意識にまかせる.
　③調節できる.
　④動きやすい..

Notes (my translation of original Japanese)

In case we have school uniforms

○ everyone is the same　no individuality

○ neat appearance

○ summer, winter　hot, cold

○ difficult to move

○ In case we have no school uniforms

　○ one's favorite appearance　individuality

　○ one's selfish appearance → leave one's consciousness

　○ adaptable

　○ easy to move

Composition

　　I think it's better if there is no uniforms. There are some advantages and disadvantages about this matter. When the students wore the uniforms, all of them look the same. They have no personality. According to my experience, the uniforms made me feel hotter in summer, colder in winter and uncomfortable especially around the neck. These are the disadvantages. But, they look OK in their uniforms. Grownups feel comfortable and say "They look like students."

　　When they don't wear the uniforms, their looks may make grownups feel uncomfortable because it's too messy and stupid for them. But, these days, there are many students wearing their uniforms messy and stupid. I think it's meaningless to wear the uniforms today.

If there was no uniforms, they could solve the problem about wearing the uniforms. Besides, they would think about what suits each of them the best. They would find the best. I think it's better than making them wear the uniforms, feel uncomfortable and look stupid.

Note: The wavy underlined parts are direct translations from the notes.

Appendix G: Notes and Compositions Written by Beni (L)

L1:
Notes

良い習慣

・自分でもクリスマスは特別な存在。
　　　　　　　　　　　　↑中

(・クリスチャンだから、という考え方は限定された考え方。

① 子供のころ 枕元にプレゼントがおいてあったとき、
（朝めがさめて）、すごく嬉しかった。

Composition
　私は<u>良い習慣</u>だと思う。それは<u>小さい頃に</u>、<u>眼がさめたらクリスマスプレゼントが置いてあった</u>という、嬉しい思い出が心の中にあるからである。またクリスマスは今の<u>自分にとっても</u>特別な日である。パーティーなど今まで特別な場所に行ったことはないけれど、これからはつき合いの中でそういう場所に行くこともあると思うし、そこで平凡な日常から離れて、楽しむことができたら非常にすばらしいことではないだろうか。
　上記にクリスチャンでもないのに...と書かれてあるが、それは<u>考え方が狭い</u>と思う。クリスチャンじゃない人とそうである人とは、クリスマスに対する考え方や姿勢など、違うと思う。クリスチャンの人は伝統的なクリスマスをすればいいし、そうでない人は自分達のやり方で、楽しむことができれば、それが一番良いと思う。

> Note: The underlined parts are verbatim copy from the notes, whereas the wavy underlined parts are paraphrases from the notes.

L2:
Notes

あったらがよい。

Because。○金がかかる、

○毎日の朝の少ない時間では、
制服があったらがよかった。

○弟 … 制服化された制服でも
<u>†かおしゃんをしている</u>。

これが私服になったら、一体どうなるのか。

○自分が今大学生になって、高校生というのは
子供であったと思う。考え方も友達に
影響されたり。まだ反抗期でもある。

Notes (my translation of original Japanese)

Better to have school uniforms

Because ○ costly

   ○ felt it better to have school uniforms in the limited time every morning.

   ○ My brother <u>makes himself fully fashionable</u> even in the constrained school uniform. If he can wear free clothing, what would happen?

   ○ Being a college student I feel now I was a child when I was a high school student. At high school age, their ways of thinking are influenced by friends and they are still in the period of rebelliousness.

Composition

I think that we had better have school clothes because at first, it cost our parents a lot of many to buy clothes, and in short time I wore it because I had a lot of homework so I stayed up late night.

    I have younger brother who is high school student, he enjoys wearing his school cloths. If he might wear his own clothes, what would happen?

    I think now that high school students are still children because they are effected their friends, 反抗する their parents. Of course because I'm college student, I thought so, when I was high school student. I didn't think so. Therefor I think that they lack their own thinking.

> Note: The wavy underlined parts are direct translations from the notes, whereas the dual underlined parts are also translations that reveal some gaps between the expressed meaning and the intended meaning exemplified in the writer's notes.

Appendix H: The Coding Categories of Introspective Reports during Pauses

Category		Definition & Examples
Planning		
Global Planning	P$_P$	Planning overall plot and content structure
		Hikari: (Me: What were you going to write?) My position is for school uniforms, so I am going to write that first. (You are going to write that.) Then I am going to write the reasons. (Reasons will follow. Have you decided what to write in the final section?) In the final section, I will make my statement once again. (Uh-huh.) So "we should do like this." (You are writing that.) Yes. (Have you decided what reasons to write?) Yes.
Local Planning	P$_L$	Planning what to write next
		Fumi: I thought I would need one more reason. (Me: Really?) In fact, I thought of stopping here. But there was too much writing space left. (Yes.) The reasons were too few, so I was thinking of another reason to write.
Idea Sorting	P$_O$	Sorting several episodes that come to the surface
		Ichiro: At first I had not decided my position (Me: Your position) yet. (You couldn't decide it easily?) No. (So you first thought of which position to take?) Yes. So for both sides, I thought of possible reasons. What kind of content came to mind if I took the positive side. Or if I took the negative side, I thought of what opposing counterparts came to mind.
Conclusion Planning	P$_C$	Planning conclusion
		Ichiro: Then I was thinking of adding one more sentence. (Me: Were you worried whether you

		should add the sentence or not?) Yes. If I stopped here, it would have been such an abrupt ending. (Then you wrote, "We regard"?) Yes. I decided to finish the final part in a general way.
Retrieval		
Retrieving Plans	**Rp**	Retrieving the plan made earlier
		Ichiro: [Referring to the main points he noted down before he wrote the first word] I was now changing the order of the points and was thinking of which one should come first.
Retrieving Information from Memory	**R**	Retrieving information that fits the plan from memory
		Ginko: I was supposed to be writing concrete examples that came from foreign countries here, so I was probably thinking of the example to write.
Generation		
Spontaneous Idea Generation	**G**	Generating what to write next spontaneously
		Ken: [After struggling] I hit on this idea at this time, and started to write it.
Idea Generation from the Text	**A**	Generating an idea related to what has been written earlier. The idea generated this way may or may not appear in the forthcoming text.
		Ken: After writing two examples following "such as," I stopped. I wanted to write the third example. (Me: Why three?) Because I thought three examples would make a good rhythm. (I see. Did the third one come out?) Yes, I wrote it.
Verbalization		
Verbalizing Propositions	**T**	Verbalizing the propositions thematized in plans into words.
		Ken: I was thinking of how to express the last sentence (Me: How to express the last sentence?) After all I wanted to say "we'd

		better have school uniforms" and I was thinking of a structure in which to express this idea.
Refining Rhetoric	L	Seeking or refining expressions rhetorically
		Fumi: At first I wrote "in the morning." But I thought this did not sound right. (Me: It did not sound right!) We are busy in the morning. So in the busy morning we don't have to choose what to wear and uniforms are convenient. (Mmm.) So I added "busy."
Correcting Surface Forms	L_L	Recalling correct surface forms or making corrections of perceived mistakes of characters or grammar
		Hikari: Here I started a sentence with "Because" with the capital letter, and saying, "Oops, I did it! I did it!" I was going to delete it.
Reader Consciousness	L_C	Devising expressions with reader consciousness
		Jiro: I might have had doubts about using the adjective "useful" here. Probably I was thinking whether this was really OK, I mean, whether the reader could understand my point by this word.
Knowledge about Composition	F	Using forms of compositions such as punctuation, paragraphing, indentation
		Ichiro: I was taught not to split a word between lines, but to begin a new line. (Me: That's right.) So I've never used hyphens in such cases. (Uh-huh) The instructor told a native-speaker student who used hyphens to stop doing that when you use handwriting. Start from the left in a new line. (So you followed the teacher's advice and moved to the next line when you were writing a long word near the end of a line.) That's right.
Rereading	E	Rereading what has been written
		Ken: [After I finished writing] I was reading the whole text to confirm whether it is coherent throughout.

Others		
Impossible to code	U	Either the writer did not remember or the coders could not categorize into any of the above
		Hikari: What was I thinking of? (Me: It was around the end of the second line.) Mmm....

Note: This is the translated version of the coding categories used in Anzai and Uchida (1981: 326). However, this is not a complete list from Anzai and Uchida (1981: 326). Only those categories coded in this study are listed here. The examples were all taken from protocol data of the present study.

Appendix I: Postwriting Questionnaire*

I. Before writing:

    1. Did you start writing right away? Yes No
    2. If your answer to Q1 is "No," what did you do? Write the kind of things you did.(e.g. I wrote down the outline. I thought what I was going to write about.)

II. In writing:

    1. How did you keep on writing? In retrospect, circle as many as apply. If you did other than given below, please specify.

    (a) I generated ideas in Japanese first, then translated them into English.
    (b) I directly wrote in English.
    (c) I wrote with the overall organization in mind.
    (d) I wrote whatever came to my mind.
    (e) I tried to write as much as possible.
    (f) I tried to write so that the sentences would flow smoothly.
    (g) When I got stuck, I stopped and thought for a while.
    (h) When I got stuck, I continued writing without stopping, and later went back to where I got stuck.
    (i) Others (Please specify)

    2. When you were writing, how much attention did you pay to the following items?

	not at all	little		fairly	very
(a) grammar	1	2	3	4	5
(b) spelling	1	2	3	4	5
(c) content	1	2	3	4	5
(d) overall organization	1	2	3	4	5
(e) vocabulary choice	1	2	3	4	5

III. After writing:

What did you do after writing? In retrospect, specify what you did after writing. (e.g., I did nothing once I finished writing. I reread to check whether the organization was appropriate or not, and revised. I added to the first version where insufficient.)

*The original version was written in Japanese. This postwriting questionnaire was originally devised for Hirose and Sasaki (1994).